P. Brosius

ACROBATS OF THE SOUL

ACROBATS OF THE SOUL

COMEDY AND VIRTUOSITY IN CONTEMPORARY AMERICAN THEATRE

RON JENKINS

THEATRE COMMUNICATIONS GROUP

Acrobats of the Soul is published by Theatre Communications Group, Inc., 355 Lexington Ave., New York, NY 10017.

The publications and programs of Theatre Communications Group are supported by Actors' Equity Foundation, Alcoa Foundation, ARCO Foundation, AT&T Foundation, Center for Arts Criticism, Citicorp/Citibank, Columbia Pictures Entertainment, Consolidated Edison Company of New York, Eleanor Naylor Dana Charitable Trust, Dayton Hudson Foundation, Exxon Corporation, Home Box Office, Japan-U.S. Friendship Commission, Jerome Foundation, Joe and Emily Lowe Foundation, Andrew W. Mellon Foundation, Mobil Foundation, National Broadcasting Company, National Endowment for the Arts, New York City Department of Cultural Affairs, New York Community Trust, New York Life Foundation, New York State Council on the Arts, Pew Charitable Trusts, Philip Morris Companies, Rockefeller Foundation, Scherman Foundation, Shell Oil Company Foundation, Shubert Foundation, L. J. Skaggs and Mary C. Skaggs Foundation, Consulate General of Spain and Xerox Foundation.

Excerpt from *Basic Intelligence* copyright © 1988 by Paul Zaloom. "Fleming's Banjo" copyright © 1988 by Stephen Wade. Excerpt from *Swimming to Cambodia* copyright © 1986 by Spalding Gray. Excerpt from *The Regard of Flight* copyright © 1986 by Bill Irwin. Excerpt from *Juggling and Cheap Theatrics* copyright © 1988 by The Flying Karamazov Brothers. Excerpt from *Penn & Teller* copyright © 1988 by Penn Gillette and Teller. All selections used by kind permission of the authors.

Front cover photograph of Bill Irwin copyright © 1988 by Jean Pagliuso.

Library of Congress Cataloging-in-Publication Data

Jenkins, Ronald Scott.
Acrobats of the soul: comedy and virtuosity in contemporary
American theatre.

1. Clowns—United States.   2. Comedians—United States.
3. Experimental theater—United States.   4. Performing arts—United
States—History—20th century.   I. Title   II. Title: Comedy and
virtuosity in contemporary American theatre.
PN1955.J46   1988   791.3'3'0973   88-12394
ISBN 0-930452-71-2
ISBN 0-930452-72-0 (pbk.)

Design by The Sarabande Press

First edition, September 1988

Con amore per la mia nonna,

Assunta Petaccio,

dolcissima farfalla della mia anima.

CONTENTS

ACKNOWLEDGMENTS

I could not have written this book without the insights of the many teachers who have helped me to understand the art of the clown. Their spirits are present between all the lines. Lou Jacobs and Hovey Burgess, who taught me about slapstick and juggling when I was a student at the Ringling Brothers Clown College. I Made Djimat and I Made Bandem, who taught me about the relationship between clowns and culture when I was apprenticed to a troupe of sacred temple dancers in Bali. Bob Butman, Sid Perloe, Paul Desjardins and Jack Coleman, who nurtured my clown troupe at Haverford College. Bob Brustein, Howard Gardner and Gerry Lesser, who deepened my understanding of the artistic process at Harvard University. Dario Fo and Franca Rame, who taught me the rhythms of comedy by allowing me to translate their plays.

I am deeply grateful to the many people who were so generous in assisting me more directly with the preparation of this book: my father, who patiently clipped out newspaper articles on artists he knew I was writing about; my brothers and sister and mother and Aunt Jo, who bolstered my sense of humor by making fun of me; Sally Schwager, who provided inspiration throughout all the stages of the project; Joel Schechter, who offered astute advice; Betty Osborn, who edited the manuscript with a deft touch; Terry Nemeth, who put together all the pieces; Laura Ross, who helped me dream it all up in the first place; Lindy Zesch, Peter Zeisler, Jim O'Quinn and Jim Leverett from Theatre Communications Group, who provided a network of contacts and support; Brigette Jennings, who helped me keep track of the Karamazovs; David White, who opened the archives of the Dance Theater Workshop to me; Judy Finelli, who kept me close to the Pickles; Jackie Liebergott, Allen Koenig, Mary Harkins and Larry Conner at Emerson College, who helped provide support for my research; Larry Eilenberg and SuAnn Hirschberg, who provided helpful California connections; John Bell, who was my liaison with the Bread and Puppet Theater; and, of course, the artists in the book, who shared their performances and thoughts with uncommon grace.

COMEDY AND SURVIVAL IN AMERICA

Clowns are kaleidoscopic emblems of human imperfection, and comedy is the chronicle of their struggle to survive. The simplest subject of farce is the man who falls down and gets up again. It wouldn't be funny if he didn't get up. We laugh, even as he lies flat on his face, because something in the clumsy dignity of his demeanor tells us that he will persevere.

Contemporary comic performers display this tenacity in unique circumstances. The forces that conspire to annihilate them reflect the complexity of our cultural environment. In addition to fighting such traditional adversaries as the pull of gravity and the constraints of authority, modern comics must confront the tyranny of mass media, technological dehumanization, political subterfuge, social alienation, rampant consumerism. Consequently they must draw on all the mental and physical resources at their disposal to emerge from the battlefield with their self-respect intact.

The comic artists profiled in this book are linked by the ingenuity with which they subversively attack the oppressive elements of everyday life in modern America. Drawing on traditions of circus, commedia dell'arte, carnival, medicine show, vaudeville, and the experimental theatre collectives of the sixties, they have developed unique forms of popular entertainment that offer audiences an exhilarating blast of comic liberation. Bill Irwin uses the eccentric dance steps of a baggy-pants hoofer to escape the clutches of a video recorder that is trying to suck him into its picture tube. Swindler illusionists, Penn and Teller expose the mechanisms of fraud by staging ironic sideshows that spoof the covert activities of stage magicians and unmask their cover-up methods of misdirection. Spalding Gray defies our reliance on mass media as the dominant source of cultural memory by recounting sharply observed stories that humorously blend his personal obsessions with the political anxieties of our times.

Much of the public's fascination with contemporary clowns is rooted in their astonishing displays of sheer skill. A host of tangible talents from juggling to banjo playing have been adopted by a new wave of performers who use them as comic survival tactics. In a high-tech society where people often feel overwhelmed by the impersonal pace of their environment, a simple act of individual virtuosity becomes a significant event, an affirmation of what a human being can accomplish without the aid of machines. This style of comedy taps into deeply ingrained American values of self-reliance.

The virtuosity of these comic performers is particularly compelling because it is presented not as an end in itself, but as a means of illuminating the conflicts between ordinary people and the forces that victimize them. Like Chaplin's underdog victories over burly policemen and Keaton's deadpan triumphs over runaway trains, the dilemmas of contemporary clowns fuel the hopes we have of solving our own most perplexing dilemmas. Mired in an avalanche of disposable consumer products, puppeteer Paul Zaloom uses the debris of American culture to create animated trash that satirizes the country's obsession with conspicuous consumption. Breaking out of the music-video aesthetics that surround him at Cirque du Soleil, physical comedian Denis Lacombe fights for his artistic integrity by conducting the music of Tchaikovsky in a grueling session of symphonic slapstick. Overcoming adversity is a theme common to all comedy, but the use of specific skills—acrobatics, dance, ventriloquism—endows these contemporary figures with genuine power.

Contributing to the audience's identification with the potency of these skilled comedians is the conscious attempt that all of them make to break down the barrier between performer and audience. Whether it is by literally inviting the spectators onto the stage or self-consciously mocking their own talents, contemporary clowns diminish the distance between themselves and their public with the egalitarian suggestion that their skills are accessible to everyone. Avner the Eccentric and the Big Apple Circus clowns involve audience volunteers in extended comic routines, setting up situations in which members of the public are sure to achieve at least a small measure of success before returning to their seats. Banjo player Stephen Wade concludes his show with a sing-along and the clowns of the Pickle Family Circus engage the audience in a game of balloon tossing. These varied forms of direct contact provide a level of intimacy rare in popular entertainment today. Saturated by overdoses of mass media, the public responds warmly to the sense of intimacy generated by these modern comic artists.

These skilled comedians also draw audiences closer by presenting themselves as fallible clowns rather than flawless superheroes. Failure is always a possibility. Whenever the Flying Karamazov Brothers drop their juggling clubs, they joke about it, calling attention to the fact that they make mistakes like everyone else. The errors are intentionally incorporated into the performance as part of the demystification of their skill. There is even a part in the show where the audience is encouraged to throw objects onto the stage that will be impossible to juggle.

If the attempt to create solidarity with the spectators links these performers to their roots in the experimental theatre of the sixties, their self-reflexive irony places them squarely in the realm of postmodern art. Another element that identifies their shows as products of the eighties is the recurring theme of power and control. The metaphors of helplessness and mastery implicit in their skill-centered comic routines are particularly trenchant in the Reagan era of trickle-down prosperity, when the ability to effect significant change in one's environment seems so elusive to so many. The contemporary clown's relatively mild handling of these issues provides a barometer of changing times. Similar themes were raised by the more militantly political clown troupes of the sixties, performing for a generation rising up in opposition to the Vietnam War. Playing to the yuppie audiences of the eighties, contemporary clowns register their protests with a diminished sense of outrage, but they still represent an anarchic alternative to the conformity of the status quo.

Historically some of the most significant recent examples of physical comedy merging with social dissent occurred in the early work of the San Francisco Mime Troupe, a fiercely political theatre company that proved to be a fruitful training ground for the future founders of the Big Apple and Pickle Family circuses, who in turn helped launch the careers of Bill Irwin and Geoff Hoyle. In the mid-sixties the Mime Troupe Americanized the masked-clown techniques of the commedia dell'arte, and offered their comic satires as a contribution to the Berkeley Free Speech Movement. In 1965 the company's founder, Ronnie Davis, was arrested for performing in San Francisco's Lafayette Park without a permit. The police took him away in mid-performance. He was wearing the mask of an Italian commedia clown, and as the authorities dragged him to the paddy wagon he shouted jokes to the audience: "Ladies and Gentlemen, Il Troupo di Mimo di San Francisco presents for your enjoyment this afternoon . . . AN ARREST!"

Davis knew that he would be arrested before he began performing. The San Francisco Parks Commission had revoked the company's permit because they found the script (*Il Candelaio* by Giordano Bruno) to be unacceptable. The Mime Troupe decided to stage the show without permission as a protest of what they considered to be a policy of State censorship. The arrest was a comic act of political defiance. Davis had arranged the staging to incorporate real policemen in the role of the clown's oppressive adversaries. Performing in the broad athletic style of commedia dell'arte, Davis created slapstick with a dangerous edge by leaping out of the policemen's reach, eluding them with sharp declamatory gestures that punctuated his satiric asides to the audience. The audience laughed at his mockery of authority and chanted their support. Many of them were prepared for the confrontation, and carried placards reading "Mime Troupe Si! Park Commission No!" Fights broke out. The public jeered the police and tried to prevent the arrest. Journalists knocked off policemen's caps in the melee. The clown's confrontation with the policemen was a concrete physicalization of the abstract tension between censorship and free speech, and the audience participated joyfully in the slapstick battle against repression.

Eventually Davis and other members of the company were brought to jail, but the public support did not end. Money for the Mime Troupe's legal defense was raised through benefit concerts, with entertainment provided by The Grateful Dead (then known as the Warlocks), The Jefferson Airplane and Lawrence Ferlinghetti. The clown's defiant posture had inspired San Francisco's seminal countercultures of psychedelic rock, beat poetry and community activists to come together for a cause that reflected their shared desires to resist the establishment and find alternative forms of power. For a moment in America's history flower power, political power and clown power crossed paths. Many arrests and trials were to follow, but eventually the right to perform in the parks without censorship was granted to all San Francisco theatre companies, and the Mime Troupe still performs every summer in Lafayette Park.

The idea of American clowns pitting their skills against the forces of social oppression can be traced back to the nineteenth century. Several decades before the Civil War a one-ring circus clown named Dan Rice set himself up as a comic adversary of big business, government corruption and cultural snobbery. Wearing a costume of red-and-white stripes that later came to be identified with the satirical cartoon figure of Uncle Sam, Rice used his skills as a mule trainer, musician and circus strongman to lampoon the social, economic and political hypocrisies of antebellum America. He named the creatures of his circus menagerie after public figures like Daniel Webster and P.T. Barnum, and staged animal acts that highlighted their namesakes' comic flaws. He was also famous for his burlesque versions of Shakespeare. In an era when America was struggling to declare its cultural independence from the dominant standards of European high art, Rice translated the bard's Elizabethan verse into frontier vernacular, and boasted that his backwoods bastardizations were superior to Shakespeare's originals. Rewriting the first scene of *Hamlet*, Rice appealed to the egalitarian values of his rural audiences by bringing the aristocratic characters down to the level of the common man: "One night two fellows standing at their post/ Beheld, my stars, a real and living ghost./ Whose ghost was this, so dismal and unhappy?/ It was, my eyes, the ghost of Hamlet's pappy!"

More than a hundred years later another company of clowns and variety artists echoed Rice's audacity by presenting a circus version of *The Comedy of Errors* at Lincoln Center. Reflecting the pulse of American culture in the eighties, they attacked Shakespeare's text with the frenetic verve of urban commandos in a postmodern jungle. The cast under the direction of Robert Woodruff included the Flying Karamazov Brothers, Avner the Eccentric, veterans of the Pickle Family Circus and hordes of stilt-walkers, plate-spinners, slap-dancers and clowns.

First produced by Gregory Mosher in 1983 at Chicago's Goodman Theatre and shown at the 1984 Olympic Arts Festival in Los Angeles, the *Comedy of Errors* seen in New York burst at the seams with the raw vitality of a quintessential American metropolis. The stage was overpopulated with break dancers, punk rockers, transvestites, jugglers, gospel singers and clowns. The heterogeneous mix of fragmented cultural icons included references to everything from Memorex and Madonna to the Iran/contra affair. Cheering the accomplishments of rap artists, unicyclists, baton twirlers and acrobats, the public expressed the same hunger for tangible exhibitions of genuine skill that sends roars through the rafters of a football stadium. The thrill of watching a performer transcend the ordinary limits of physical possibility generates an exhilaration that stage acting rarely evokes.

The Elizabethan eloquence of Shakespeare's verse was replaced with a distinctively American lyricism that sacrificed subtleties of syntax to the crude kinetic poetry of body shapes and flying objects. Using their physical skills to create visual metaphors for their characters' intentions, the performers attempted to integrate the art of the actor with the art of the athlete. Angry wives hurled knives at husbands whose backs were literally up against the wall. Jealous rage was expressed in the furious twirling of a majorette's baton. Precarious relationships were developed as lovers walked a tightrope. Though their verbal dexterity did not match the sophistication of their physical skills, the performers' double-edged efforts suggested the unfulfilled possibility of the actor as an acrobat of the soul.

In its use of popular-entertainment skills to revitalize classic texts for American audiences, this *Comedy of Errors* is consistent with populist experiments of innovative theatre artists from around the world. Bertolt Brecht was influenced by the techniques of German cabaret clown Karl Valentin. Jean Cocteau engaged the Fratellini Circus Clowns for one of his plays. The Russian experimentalist Vsevelod Meyerhold used a troupe of Chinese jugglers in one of his productions and staged another with a Harlequin character performing a highwire ballet.

Meyerhold was rebelling against the emotional realism of Stanislavsky's work at the Moscow Art Theatre, and wanted to create a form of expression based on musical, gestural and visual rhythms rather than naturalistic logic. He embraced the concrete skills and broad physical acting of circus, commedia dell'arte and Russian vaudeville as the cornerstone of his approach. In 1912 Meyerhold wrote:

"The juggler reveals the total self-sufficiency of the actor's skill with the expressiveness of his gestures and the language of his movements."

American experimental theatre troupes of the sixties and early seventies pursued an aesthetic that was similar to Meyerhold's in its rejection of realism and reliance on physical acting. Some turned to the popular entertainment forms of commedia dell'arte and circus. After performing with the San Francisco Mime Troupe for several years, Larry Pisoni, Peggy Snider, Michael Christensen and Paul Binder branched off to create performing troupes that celebrated pure physical performance skill. Pisoni and Snider founded the Pickle Family Circus in San Francisco, while Binder started New York's Big Apple Circus with Christensen as his star clown. Vermont's Bread and Puppet Theater, which nurtured the performance skills of puppeteer-minimalist Paul Zaloom, created avant-garde political theatre rooted in European traditions of pageantry and folk puppets. In New York, Richard Schechner's Performance Group (which eventually evolved into the Wooster Group) experimented with environmental staging that created a carnival spirit by incorporating audiences into the setting of the plays. Adopting a Brechtian fairground aesthetic that blurred the boundaries between audience and actor as well as between the actor and his role, the Performance Group gave monologist Spalding Gray the opportunity to develop the self-reflexive acting techniques that he uses in his autobiographical memory plays. Herbert Blau's KRAKEN was another company that searched for new forms of physical theatre. Bill Irwin's work with KRAKEN eventually led him to seek circus training at the Ringling Brothers Clown College. Established in 1967 by the Ringling Brothers Circus, Clown College attracted scores of young performers dissatisfied with traditional theatre, among them Penn Jillette, whose love of the carnival sideshow was incorporated into the innovative comedy of *Penn & Teller*.

Like Meyerhold, Brecht, Cocteau and the experimentalists of American avant-garde theatre, the comic artists featured in this book cannot fit their performances into the preexisting categories of traditional theatre. Inspired by popular entertainment skills that defy the rules of conventional drama, they have invented their own idiosyncratic forms of comedy. Some of them have been labeled "New Vaudevillians," but most reject the term as a meaningless phrase that has little to do with their artistic goals or origins. If there is anything that unites these disparate innovators, it is their respect for sheer skill and its creative applications to the art of comedy. All of them have spent years perfecting particular talents, but choose to underplay their virtuosity by making it a source of self-satire. In an age of diminishing expectations their humor reflects the ironic underside of America's obsession with power and control.

These contemporary clowns explore the issues of failure and success at their most basic level of physical reality. Their displays of virtuosity are executed in a comic struggle with allegorical adversaries that plague us all. Bill Irwin relies on his rubber-limbed agility to save him from an unseen force that threatens to suck him off the stage and out of existence. Spalding Gray's weapon against the oblivion of being forgotten is his ability to sculpt memories into a rapid-fire barrage of autobiographical stories. Penn and Teller undermine the perpetration of deception by using their considerable skills as stage magicians to dismantle the mechanisms of illusion. Ventriloquist Paul Zaloom sidesteps the suffocating effects of consumerism by giving voices of satiric protest to discarded products of the material world. Stephen Wade rescues faded folklore and backwoods musicians from the shadows of history by resurrecting them with the talking steel strings of his banjo. Avner the Eccentric defuses the loneliness of a one-man clown show by shrewdly involving the audience in his onstage antics. The Flying Karamazov Brothers tackle the laws of entropy with demonstrations of team juggling. The Big Apple clowns whittle down the distance between the haves and the have-nots by mocking the stars of the circus with parodies of physical overachievement. Denis Lacombe overcomes the alienation of life in a high-tech circus with comic exhibitions of physical excess. And the Pickle Family Circus does its best to reverse the fragmentation of modern society by inviting the audience to join an extended family of acrobats, gorillas and clowns united by the simple pleasure of working together towards a common goal.

In their own ways all these performers use specialized skills to overcome restrictions imposed by society, gravity, logic and convention. Refusing to submit to the tyrannies of high-tech consumerism, bureaucratic doubletalk or political duplicity, this battalion of acrobats, jugglers and illusionists embodies our fundamental aspirations for dignity and freedom. Their complex forms of comic virtuosity hint at a fragile relationship between clowns and power that links our hunger for laughter with our instinct to survive.

ACROBATS OF THE SOUL

PAUL ZALOOM

"My goal is to write a very funny piece of work that relates directly to the survival of the audience. Ideally the public will laugh hard, have a great time, and leave the theatre thoroughly refreshed and yet deeply disturbed about our mutual fate."

—PAUL ZALOOM

Packing crates. TV antennas. Cotton balls. Old newspapers. Automobile parts. Plastic forks. Paul Zaloom collects the debris of American culture and sculpts it into a theatre of trash. He animates the objects he finds with multitonal voices. Cigars speak in the gruff mutterings of Congressmen in caucus. Sheets of wrinkled black plastic hiss like acid rain. And a tiny black reading lamp takes on the sinister accent of a KGB agent. Zaloom grabs one piece of junk after another, sets it onto his table, gives it a voice, then hurls it to the floor. His images dissolve into one another with an anarchic velocity that heightens their comic punch. By the time his performance ends, he is standing in a garbage dump of discarded characters, like a crazed television game-show host in the aftermath of a marathon prize giveaway.

Zaloom uses the paraphernalia of our consumer culture to create a satiric microcosm of the American landscape. With his nonstop patter and frenetic enthusiasm Zaloom is a modern-day carnival barker, a medicine-show pitchman who uses irony to sell a vision of a nation being consumed by its own refuse. Zaloom has perfected the art of postmodern ventriloquism. Duchamp put a urinal in a museum and called it a "Fountain." Zaloom would have gone one step further, and made the urinal sing and dance. His readymade puppets transform society's waste products into entertaining commentary on society's wastefulness. In Zaloom's skillful hands, found objects take on a manic life of their own, and hurtle through their dialogue with an intensity that mirrors the high-speed environment they depict.

Born in Brooklyn and raised on Long Island, Zaloom spent much of his childhood collecting garbage. He put some of his best junk on display for the neighbors in a trash museum that he set up in the family garage, but it wasn't until Zaloom arrived at Goddard College in Vermont that he discovered a theatrical use for garbage. Under the influence of the Bread and Puppet Theater, who were in residence at Goddard, Zaloom began turning still-life piles of debris into animated theatrical trash. He was so impressed with the company's epic style of

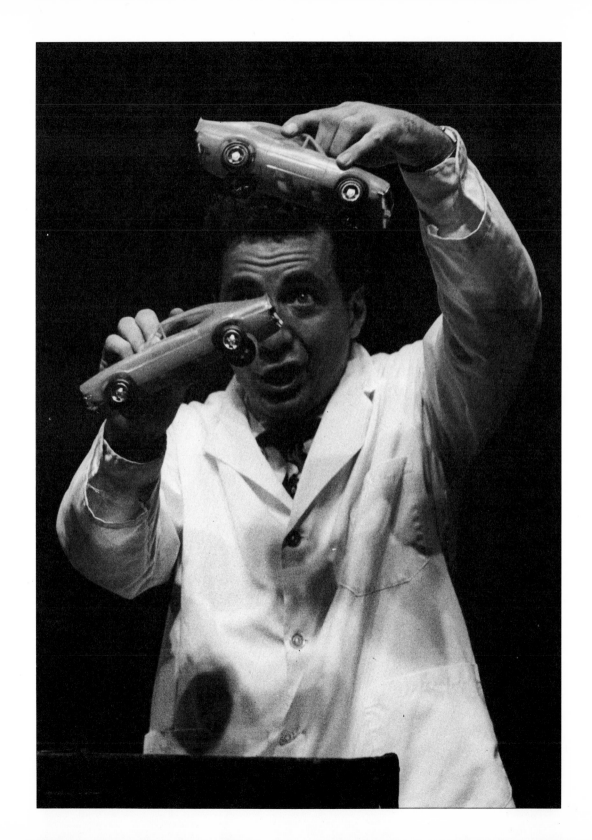

"TELEVISION IN
AMERICA," A SEGMENT
OF THE FUTURE.

political puppetry that he joined them as an apprentice performer on their 1971 European tour. One of the pieces he performed with them was an adaptation of a traditional Japanese Kyogen play called *The Birdcatcher in Hell*. Bread and Puppet adapted the story to portray hell as the My Lai massacre in Vietnam.

From 1973-77, while working full time with Bread and Puppet's director Peter Schumann, Zaloom began developing an aesthetic of his own. He took Schumann's style of rural European folk art and adapted it to fit the claustrophobic energy of urban America. In Schumann's Vermont spectacles twenty-foot-high puppets perform on a fifteen-acre meadow as audiences watch from a natural hillside amphitheatre. From Schumann, Zaloom learned how to populate an entire environment with animated objects, but he chose to reduce the dimensions of his puppet universe to a miniature scale and inhabit it with artificial rather than natural materials. Schumann makes his art of of found materials, transforming them into shapes that echo the beauty of their natural settings. Zaloom prefers to leave his ready-made objects in the pristine state of junkiness in which he found them. Influenced by the manic jazz poetry of Lord Buckley, Zaloom added a comic soundtrack to his performances that contrasts to the slow-paced music and dialogue used by Bread and Puppet. Like Buckley, who performed in the thirties, forties and fifties, Zaloom uses his voice to create layers of rapidly changing aural effects that capture the frenetic pace of city life.

New York, New York is representative of the solo shows Zaloom began creating in 1977, when he started working independently of Bread and Puppet. This short play is a tabletop vision of New York City. The skyline is made out of white styrofoam packing products. The traffic jam is a line-up of transistor radios, tiny yellow cowboy hats (the cabs) and a remote-control channel changer. A chisel banging up and down on the table marks a construction site. Zaloom brings the scene to life with a collage of vocal sound effects. He honks, curses, shouts and mutters a multitude of complaints. When an accident occurs, Zaloom warbles the shrill wail of an ambulance siren and a Band-Aid box rolls onto the scene.

Zaloom's New York is a throwaway city of disembodied voices, teeming with frustrations, precariously balanced on the edge of self-destruction. The discardable materials with which he constructs his miniature metropolis are a measure of its impermanence; they are also a reminder of the poverty of its inhabitants. The subway is a tube full of dirt that gets thrown back and forth from one end to the other. Dilapidated cardboard cartons stand in for the slums of South Bronx. Politicians who arrive in the projects to proclaim their support for the poor are fashioned out of fancier objects that clearly belong to a more opulent world. Mayor Koch is a painted toy horse. Senator D'Amato is a shiny apple. The governor is a bottle of soda pop. Soon an ominous black briefcase hovers over the table, signaling the arrival of the Presidential helicopter. The briefcase never lands, but Zaloom pulls out a copy of *Newsweek* with Reagan's photo on the cover, just long enough for the chief to say "No" and fly away from the unsightly mess.

Zaloom also gives a voice to the forgotten poor of the Lower East Side, who are evicted from their flimsy paper houses by a sock-puppet slum landlord. The tenant dolls are made of fragile bits of newspaper that float noiselessly to the ground when the landlord rips off the cardboard wall of their building and shakes them violently out of their homes. It is like a Punch and Judy show in which grotesque acts of violence are perpetrated against the tenants by a slapstick figure of greed. After the eviction the miniscule living cubicles are reduced to half their size and sold as luxury condominiums. Zaloom's disposable props are an appropriate metaphor for this scenario of shoddy construction and instant profits.

Every so often the noisy hubbub slows down, and Zaloom holds a gun and a thick wad of dollar bills in suspension over his city of trash. The surreal image unifies the chaotic urban activity that has been transpiring beneath it. Violence and money explain everything. Motivation for the construction, destruction and furious motion of everything in Zaloom's junkyard metropolis can be traced back to a dollar bill or a gun. Zaloom makes no comment. He simply stops the action and holds the objects up for our inspection. As usual, he stands in full view of the

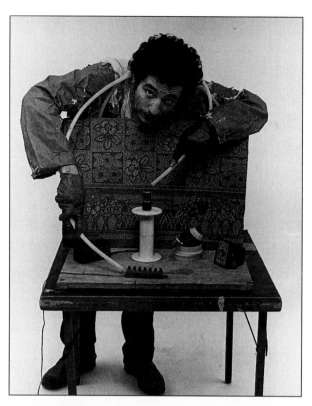
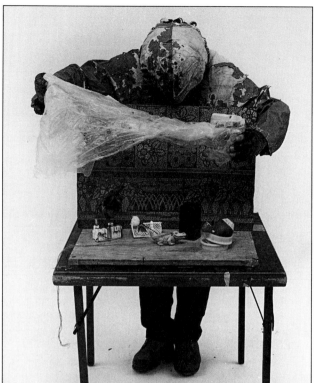

audience while performing, but the simplicity of his presentation renders him almost invisible. Zaloom is without question the guiding spirit behind everything that is seen, but his juxtapositions of images are so striking that his props compel more attention than he does. Through a complex pattern of vocal changes and physical gestures Zaloom gives the illusion of life to inanimate objects that are shrewdly selected to satirize the subjects being discussed. The animator recedes into the background, but his point of view is clearly discernible from the choices he has made about which bits of debris to rescue from the garbage.

Zaloom has based numerous routines on documents he has obtained from government offices. In a piece entitled *Do It Now* Zaloom presents a detailed description of the civil defense authority's plans for evacuating America's urban population in the event of a nuclear attack. He displays the original brochures and diagrams from government printing presses, in addition to highlighting bits of information with cartoon drawings of his own. A house covered with mounds of dirt illustrates the government's advice on protecting your home from radioactive fallout. Zaloom has used the government's figures to calculate that twenty thousand buckets full of dirt are all it takes to make the average family home completely radiation proof. The brochures also recommend that people take their credit cards with them when they evacuate. And citizens are reassured that companies like American Express and Pizza Hut have duplicates of their records stored in underground silos so that they can continue to serve their customers in the postnuclear era. The assumption underlying all the advice is that atomic war will be conducted in a calm and orderly fashion. The black humor of Zaloom's routine is heightened by the realization that everything he says is taken directly from government handouts. Zaloom's garbage-cluttered America is hurtling towards self-annihilation, and his presentation of the civil defense documents suggests that the government printing offices are generating reams of trash designed to placate the populace into believing that the apocalypse will be as painless as a well-planned trip to the shopping mall.

AN EARLY WORK, THE WORLD OF PLASTIC.

Although Zaloom performs regularly in theatres around the country and has appeared frequently on television, he returns every summer to Vermont to play the role of the ringmaster in Bread and Puppet's annual *Domestic Resurrection Circus*. He also performs his solo pieces as part of the circus "Sideshows." Zaloom's ingenious use of perspective can be seen most clearly in a situation like this, where his miniature worldview is juxtaposed against Schumann's giant images. In the 1987 circus Bread and Puppet commemorated the two-hundredth anniversary of the U.S. Constitution with a huge spectacle that featured hundreds of puppets and dozens of puppeteers. In his role as ringmaster Zaloom led a marching band onto the field, followed by a parade of schoolbuses, motorcycles, pickup trucks and a bicycle built for two. The vehicles were presented as ani-

ZALOOM AS THE RINGMASTER OF BREAD AND PUPPET'S DOMESTIC RESURRECTION CIRCUS.

mated characters in the circus, but the central figures were larger-than-life puppets of the Founding Fathers, who try to build a Constitution conducive to "life, liberty, and the pursuit of property."

Zaloom's miniature sideshow, performed in an adjoining pine forest before the large circus began, is also a satire on America's obsession with the acquisition of property, but his play is set in the 1980s in the Lower East Side of New York. The central character, an impoverished artist named Leonardo, is being evicted from his apartment so that the landlord can sell it as a condo. Now that East Village property values have gone up, the landlord advises Leonardo to move on to some other run-down neighborhood to fulfill the artist's true role in American society as a "Mobile Urban Renewal Unit." For his stage, Zaloom constructed a model of an apartment building just large enough to cover him as he manipulates the hand-puppet characters from behind it. He has transplanted a piece of Manhattan to the wilds of Vermont and inhabited it with landlords, analysts, city marshals and new-wave artists constructed out of fragments of urban debris. Leonardo's dog is a dust mop and his mother's hair is a steel-wool wig that enables her to clean her son's dishes by rubbing her head in them.

A few hours later Zaloom performs in the main circus, where the play of perspectives is reversed. Everything is larger than life, and as many as ten performers can be required to animate a single puppet. When the Founding Fathers write the Constitution, the "living document" is represented as a giant cardboard baby. Zaloom narrates, and puppeteers add body parts that match America's system of government. The judiciary is "the long arm of the law." Freedom of speech is a pair of lips. And the right to privacy is a fig leaf between the baby's legs. Zaloom had used a similar device in miniature for another of his shows, in which a TV anchorman accompanies news of world disasters by mutilating the limbs of a paper doll, but for the outdoor circus the animated body politic is big enough to project its satiric message to several thousand people sitting on a hillside. The scale has shifted from Zaloom's compact portable television to

"LEONARDO'S REVENGE" FROM CREATURE FROM THE BLUE ZALOOM.

Schumann's expansive drive-in movie, but the satiric impulse and the imaginative use of object representation are clearly born out of the same aesthetics.

Schumann deflates American political mythology in a cow pasture. Zaloom punctures the same myths on a tabletop. Their visions overlap and intersect, while maintaining their separate identities. Zaloom expresses his distinctive vision of the country as a wasteland most completely in a piece called *In America*. As is true of his other works, *In America* was performed in New York and on tour, but it acquired a more complex resonance when presented as part of the densely leveled *Resurrection Circus* in 1986. The theme of that year's circus was hunger. Schumann used museum exhibits, pageants, lectures and puppet shows of various sizes to stress the irony of America's unevenly distributed wealth. He stated his

theme as "the hunger of the hungry and the hunger of the overfed." Zaloom's play contributed to the theme with an incisive series of vignettes that satirize aspects of American life, among them farming, education, communication, prison, eating.

As the ringmaster in the outdoor circus, Zaloom had introduced "the death-defying tightrope act of dairy farming in Vermont." The act pitted farmers and their puppet cows against government agents who drove up in a 1968 Oldsmobile and attacked them with signs reading "Property Taxes," "Low Milk Prices" and "Dairy Termination Program." The farmers united to chase away their adversaries, and the victory was celebrated by a dance of eighteen-foot-high farm couples. When Zaloom performed his own show, the segment called "Farming in America" dealt with the same conflict using household items as the principal players. The dairy farmhouse was a school lunchpail, and the nearby silo was a thermos. The farmers were garden tools and the dairy herd was made of pint-sized milk cartons painted with the black-and-white patterns of Holstein cows. The government representative was a plastic fist with an extended middle finger who assured the farmers he was giving their problems serious consideration, but his visit was followed immediately by the bankers in the form of a toy safe who repossessed the farm, silo and cows, and left the farmers in an empty field. "And that's farming in America," concluded Zaloom darkly, moving on quickly to another topic. There was no happy ending as there was in Schumann's circus. Zaloom uses the household products of consumer wealth to tell the story of people who are being shut out of prosperity. In the theatre of trash the problems of the hungry are animated by the leftovers of the overfed.

One segment of *In America* makes the overfed the direct target of its satire. In "Eating in America," yuppies going out to dinner are played by clear plastic champagne glasses. They drive up in a Volvo, portrayed by a silver tray. Their maître d' is a bottle of expensive wine who speaks with a French accent. At first he informs the yuppies that there will be a two-hour wait for a table, but when they plaster a dollar bill onto his label, he finds them a table immediately, and pours

THE FARM CRISIS SEQUENCE FROM IN AMERICA.

them drinks. An unwanted visitor who clearly cannot afford to eat at the restaurant arrives, announcing "I am hungry." The intruder, a lowly Styrofoam cup, is immediately crushed by the wine bottle for not conforming to the dress code. Meanwhile the yuppies get drunk, eat rich French cooking, and die from high-cholesterol heart attacks. "And that's eating in America," declares Zaloom as he clears the table, adding the refuse from this routine to the growing pile of junk on the floor.

As Zaloom continues his performance, the accumulation of debris around him acquires its own momentum. His vocal rhythms build to increasingly frantic climaxes as each new item speaks with a voice of its own. One after another he pulls plastic products from bags and stacks them onto his table as if he were promoting a surrealistic clearance sale. Zaloom has created a new form of American theatre by giving narrative structure to the fruits of a random shopping spree. He encourages us to look at his purchases from perspectives that reveal their significance as cultural icons. In "Education in America" the schoolteacher is portrayed by a plastic bottle of dishwashing liquid. Never has the cultural stereotype implicit in the product's packaging been made more clear. Zaloom animates "Miss Joy" with a matronly voice, and the shape of the bottle is a perfect plastic replica of the kind of large-breasted, big-hipped woman society assumes will be teaching in elementary schools or washing the dishes at home.

The Vermont version of *In America* was performed in an old barn that Schumann has converted into a puppet museum, housing hundreds of papier-mâché figures that Bread and Puppet have used in performance over the past twenty years. Schumann endows his puppets with a simple humanity that comes from a tradition of folk art. The Bread and Puppet figures of children, farmers, working people and animals provide a poignant backdrop for Zaloom's theatre of trash. Schumann's puppets are the victims of the mass-production ethic that Zaloom is satirizing. They are suspended from the ceiling, hung from the walls, and attached to the old wooden beams that support the barn's sagging floor. The

earth-toned puppets are crying, drowning, thinking, praying and milking cows. With their bulbous pastel faces and burlap bodies, Schumann's creations are like a new species of pathetic animated potatoes miraculously given the ability to think and feel.

Zaloom gives a voice to the downtrodden souls that Schumann visualizes so powerfully, but he purposefully denies them a face. His puppets are the impersonal products of bargain basements and discount shopping centers, instant characters made from artificial ingredients. In one of Zaloom's routines he details multiple uses of Wonder Bread that range from cleaning to clothing, but do not include nourishment. Schumann, by contrast, personally bakes hundreds of loaves of sourdough rye bread to give away to spectators at the *Domestic Resurrection Circus*. The baking of the bread in large outdoor mud hearths is part of Schumann's domestic resurrection that will combat the evils of famine, poverty and war. Every year the circus concludes with a flaming ritual exorcism of the forces of evil. In 1987 the military-industrial complex was set on fire by an earth-mother puppet whose embrace was over fifty feet wide. In 1986 the ghoulish specter of hunger was burnt to ashes in the middle of Bread and Puppet's green pasture.

Zaloom does not offer such pastoral visions of hopefulness. He portrays America as a consumer paradise in which the products and the people are interchangeably disposable. When the Soviet Union sends submarines to spy on the heart of capitalism, Zaloom imagines a vacuum-cleaner nozzle emerging from the depths to suck up the dust from a colored wall map of the U.S. The nozzle moves across one state after another, as if everything worth knowing about the country could be assimilated like so much lint. *In America* closes with a vision of prison inmates as equally discardable commodities. Zaloom's junkyard image for an American prison is a birdcage full of rubber bands with two oversized metal corkscrews inserted between the bars. The inmates have tried to revolt in protest of their overcrowded conditions, but the cork-

screw guards are quelling the rebellion with violent measures of repression.

The intentional cheapness of Zaloom's aesthetics has a sharp satiric bite. His timing is upbeat. His tone is reassuring. His smile is bright. But Zaloom's optimism is as hollow as the sales pitch of a television ad man. He manipulates objects as skillfully and cynically as advertisers manipulate their target audiences. Zaloom's style of trash-dump ventriloquism mirrors the political and commercial ventriloquism of a culture in which people are paid to say things they don't believe. Forgoing the dummy of the traditional ventriloquist, Zaloom uses a bargain basement full of animated objects to suggest that the unquestioning consumer is America's real dummy. Like an old-fashioned department-store floor-walker, Zaloom cheerfully ushers his audience into oblivion, as if it were just another end-of-the-season sale.

From *Basic Intelligence*

Dressed in a pinstripe suit, Zaloom projects slides of U.S. Government documents and publications while delivering the following narration.

Good evening, ladies and gentlemen. My name is Paul Zaloom, and I am one of the eighty-five thousand new civilian employees hired by the Pentagon since President Reagan came into office seven years ago. Tonight I'm going to present to you what is really a combination of information and performance. Some people call that an *informance*; I like to call it a *perforation*.

Tonight's perforation is essentially a book report: I'm going to be showing you three books that you can purchase from the U.S. Government Printing Office book catalog that can give you an idea of what's going on in the U.S. military establishment today. The first book from the catalog we're going to look at is this Joint Chiefs of Staff/Department of Defense *Dictionary of Military and Associated Terms*. With this dictionary, you too can comprehend some of the jargonization that has occurred in the vernacularizing process in military vocabularization. I'd like to show you some sample definitions from the dictionary if I could:

nominal weapon—a nuclear weapon producing a yield of approximately 20 kilotons.

disaffected person—a person who is alienated or estranged from those in authority or has a lack of loyalty for the government; a state of mind.

There are some words in the dictionary that clearly will not be useful to you as civilian personnel. Here's an excellent example:

acoustic warfare counter-countermeasures—acoustic warfare counter-countermeasures involve anti-acoustic warfare support measures and anti-acoustic warfare countermeasures and may or may not involve underwater acoustic emissions.

You can see what I mean right there. There are also some words in the dictionary that have been singled out as "not to be used" by military personnel. Let's have a quick look at some of the forbidden words:

local war—not to be used; see limited war.

spasm war—not to be used; see general war.

limited denied war—not to be used; no substitute recommended.

all-out war—not to be used; see general war.

accidental war—not to be used; see accidental attack.

total nuclear war—not to be used; see general war.

Here's a word we can use:

gross error—a nuclear weapon detonation at such a distance from the desired ground zero as to cause no nuclear damage to the target.

A gross error. Well, that's the first book in the catalog.

I'd like to address the next section of the perforation to the business persons in the audience. I urge you to purchase this book, *Selling to the Military*, from the Department of Defense. With this booklet, you can find out to whom you can sell your goods or services in the U.S. military. I'd like to quickly show you how you'd use this reference. Let's say you are in manufacturing; you manufacture . . . whips and harnesses, for example. Well, if you turn to page 65, you'll find the Defense Construction Supply Center in Columbus, Ohio, purchases "harnesses, whips, and related animal furnishings." Turn the page, and you'll learn that the supply center at 700 Robbins Avenue in Philadelphia purchases "shackles and slings." If you're in the heaviest bondage thing of all, turn to page 57 and contact the San Antonio Air Logistics Center in Texas because they procure "nuclear bombs, nuclear projectiles, nuclear warheads and warhead sections, nuclear demolition charges, nuclear rockets . . ." et cetera, et cetera. San Antonio is also in charge of procuring "miscellaneous waxes, oils, and fats," so if you have any of those lying around your basement or garage, contact San Antonio.

All right, you've just sold to the Pentagon. But what about buying from the military? You need this booklet—*How to Buy Surplus Personal Property from the Department of Defense*. On page 5, you can find out how to buy back those "oils and waxes" you just sold to the Pentagon. Also on page 5, learn how you can purchase "explosives," even "guided missile equipment." But perhaps you need a place to store your new guided missile equipment. I have an idea from this little green book:

> The General Services Administration is responsible for the disposal of all government owned surplus real property, including . . . missile silos.

You simply purchase a silo and stick the guided missile in there.

A lot of people, when they hear the word *surplus*, the first thing that comes to their minds is: jeeps. Unfortunately, the jeeps that the military manufactures today are not appropriate for civilian use on our nation's highways.

> Accordingly, these vehicles must be mutilated by cutting the three rear differential mounting pads out of the body frame and the body completely cut and severed at a point near the center of the vehicle. This is a safety requirement.

On page 6, there is a complete list of the materials the Pentagon manufactures more of than anything else. I'm talking, of course, of "scrap and waste: film, food waste, metals, oil, paper, rubber, testiles . . . ." Testiles? Wow, what a typo! A "gross error"!

Well, I certainly have enjoyed interfacing with you tonight. Let's touch base again sometime. Thank you, and good night.

—*Paul Zaloom*

Stephen Wade

"When I first heard the five-string banjo it was a world of sound. Down low it could bark, and up high it'd be like bells. It could be strident and then whisper. It could be plaintive and mournful and then explosively articulate. It's like watercolors. It's full of happy accidents. It's free. You can improvise with it. It's asymmetrical and it's interesting to look at. It has personality. It's eccentric. It's hard to tune. It's recalcitrant. It's like a musical mule."

—STEPHEN WADE

Stephen Wade doesn't just play songs on his banjo. He plays history. Wade's five-string partner is animated by the ghosts of all the people whose songs and stories appear in his show. On a trip to Cherry Log, Georgia, Wade learned a tune from a man named Chesley Chancey. "He was nearly eighty years old when he taught it to me," says Wade in the introduction to the piece. His shaggy curls fall over his face as he bows his head in an unforced display of affection for his teacher. "It was the oldest song he knew and he learned it from his grandfather." Wade plays the song with such crisp authenticity that you can practically see the clearing in the woods where the two of them sat down to play together. "That's 'Mulberry Gap' from Chesley Chancey," Wade reminds us when he's finished, as if Chesley's name were part of the song's title, and hearing it had put us all on intimate terms with the Georgia banjo player and the place he called home.

Wade is an oral historian who passes on his stories in syncopated prose, but he isn't content simply to set America's past to music. He makes history hoot, holler and stomp its feet. When Wade talks about Mississippi River steamboats, he picks at the banjo with his left hand, sets up a driving rhythm by tapping his feet, imitates the engine bells with his voice, and moves his right arm in wide circles that represent the turning of the forty-foot paddle wheel. The steel-string music races along like water splashing against the side of the boat. If you never get to ride on a Mississippi riverboat, the next best thing is to listen to Stephen Wade play one on his banjo.

The banjo is a quintessentially American instrument, ideally suited to catch the frenetic cadences of the country's character. The restless energy of banjo music captures the heartbeat of a society in a state of perpetual motion. Wade shrewdly exploits the banjo's inherent theatrical qualities, using its eccentric sound patterns to accompany his equally eccentric stories about people who embody the nation's comic heritage of salesmanship, showmanship and one-upmanship. He uses variations of fast-paced strumming as acoustic correlatives for making a sale, straining to be noticed, or trying to outdo a competitor. His music also taps the kinetic joy of his characters' successes and the twanging sadness of their disappointments.

Drawing his texts from old newspapers, novels, legends and folklore, Wade has created a unique form of musical storytelling by using the banjo to express the emotional intensity of the situations he recounts. Wade's vocal delivery is nearly deadpan, and his face, though sensitive, is almost expressionless. All the excitement in the stories is provided by the sounds of the banjo. The strings squeal with pleasure, howl with astonishment, and mutter with suspicion, while Wade leans over his instrument and cradles it like a mother encouraging her baby to speak.

The songs, stories and jokes that Wade coaxes out of his talking banjo are like the family album of the extended clan that Wade gathered around him as he learned his craft. Each musical riff or verbal punch line is an affectionate tribute to Wade's teachers, and his teachers' teachers, tracing a trail back to the nineteenth century. Fleming Brown, the banjo player who taught at the Old Town School of Folk Music in Chicago, was the most direct influence on Wade's music. The Old Town School was only a few blocks from the neighborhood where Wade grew up, and he began studying there in 1971 after discovering Brown's illustrations in a book about banjo playing written by Pete Seeger. While Brown's music was partially shaped by his admiration for Seeger, his ear for storytelling was sharpened by his contact with oral historian Studs Terkel, who was the M.C. of a folk band that Brown played with in the fifties. Brown's connection to comedy and storytelling also grows out of the radio show he hosted with Mike Nichols, then with Second City, at WFMT, the same station that produces Terkel's radio work. The president of WFMT, Ray Nordstrand, is the man Wade credits for first giving him the idea to put together his one-man hodgepodge of oral-archeological-historical-ethnomusicological folklore. Entitled *Banjo Dancing*, the show premiered at Chicago's Body Politic Theatre in 1979, moved to Broadway in 1980, and is currently playing at Washington's Arena Stage, where it opened in 1981. It is the longest running theatrical presentation in that city's history.

Although *Banjo Dancing* was born on the North Side of Chicago, its roots run deep into the musical and oral traditions of the American South. Wade's teacher, Fleming Brown, spent a long time studying banjo with Doc Hopkins, who grew up in Possum Hollow, Kentucky, and started his musical career playing the banjo for a medicine show run by a man named Dakota Jack. Hopkins would play a song about Jesse James to draw a crowd and Dakota Jack would talk them into buying shampoos and liniments which he promised would cure just about everything that ailed them. Wade met Hopkins in the early seventies and performed with him in pizza parlors and college campuses around the Chicago area. When Hopkins got too old and weak to play his banjo, he continued teaching Wade new songs by whistling them from his bed.

Wade's respect for Doc Hopkins' music is reflected in almost all the music he plays, and Hopkins' medicine-show background winds its way obliquely into *Banjo Dancing* when Wade performs the poetic sales patter of a ballpoint-pen vendor. The text was transcribed from a recording of a New York City street hawker made in 1952, but the rolling alliteration and smooth-flowing superlatives of the speech echo the alluringly slick rhythms of a rural medicine-show pitchman. "Here's a pen that slides and glides over your paper just like a ball of marble over a sheet of glass . . . a purple polyglot pen . . . writes in all languages . . . removes spots, stains, corns and calluses . . . don't hesitate . . . poets of the world ignite . . . ." The medicine-show motif is further strengthened by the fact that Wade is actually out in the audience selling pens as he performs the pitch. He has previously persuaded the audience to take quarters out of their pockets to tap along to the beat of the banjo, and while their money is conveniently located in their outstretched hands Wade pulls a pen out of his pocket and asks innocently, "Does anybody want to buy a pen? It's only a quarter."

The first sale transpires almost before the bewildered spectator in the front row

knows what is happening. Wade gives her a pen, holds up his newly acquired quarter, and caps off the transaction with a proud punch line that could compete with "E pluribus unum" as the national motto: "The best time to make a sale is when you've got a customer." The audience laughs at his disarmingly honest salesmanship and happily trades dozens of quarters for dozens of pens. Wade's patter, punctuated by lively licks on the banjo, keeps them laughing and buying until almost everyone in the theatre has purchased a souvenir, and Wade has amassed a piggy bank full of quarters. The musical shopping spree occurs early in the show, creating a bond between Wade and his audience that grows stronger as his performance continues. He has made physical contact with most of the people in the room. They have all actively participated in a communal event, tapping quarters to the music and laughing together as they exchanged them for pens. Numbed by the slick advertising techniques of the mass media, the public is delighted to be reminded for a moment of the way business might have been conducted by a traveling Yankee peddlar or the joke-telling proprietor of a small-town general store.

If Wade's performance of the pen pitch is haunted by the ghosts of Dakota Jack's Kentucky medicine show, his toe-tapping rendition of the "spectacular and death-defying high diver extraordinary" is inhabited by a different crowd of patron spirits. The tall tale of a rivalry between two high divers who work for competing carnivals was told to Wade by Jack Conroy, an eighty-nine-year-old writer who collected oral histories for the Federal Writers project in the 1930s. Conroy grew up in a mining town in rural Missouri, but spent time in Chicago, where he heard the high-diving story from a retired circus strongman in the King's Palace Bar on North Clark Street. The banjo music Wade uses to animate the story is full of melodies he learned to play in the same Chicago neighborhood where the old circus veteran entertained his drinking partners with the far-fetched fable of life on a circus sideshow. Like the story, the tunes had traveled a long circuitous road from the rural frontier to an urban center.

The tall tale revolves around two performers' ongoing attempts to outdo each other. The narrator is known professionally as "Billy the Dolphin" and prides himself on being able to dive from enormous heights into incredibly shallow water. He began his career, he says, as a child leaping off silos into the dew on the grass. "Didn't even muss my hair," he boasts with the low-keyed bravado typical of tall-tale heroes from Paul Bunyan to Davy Crockett. Billy's rival, Eddie Labrine, bills himself as "the human seal," and kindles Billy's competitive spirit by diving from progressively higher towers into increasingly shallower pools. Eventually Billy injures himself in an attempt to dive from a thousand feet into a damp bath mat. He claims he would have pulled off the stunt with no problem if his rival hadn't sneaked into the carnival grounds before the show and wrung the bath mat dry.

The wry and playful tone of exaggeration at the heart of the story is captured perfectly by the vibrant frailing of Wade's banjo. Tall tales were a vital form of nineteenth-century American humor, mirroring the overinflated confidence of a nation in the process of conquering what seemed a limitless wilderness. Severed from the cultural conditions that gave birth to their peculiar brand of whimsy, these same tall tales often fall flat when retold in modern circumstances. Wade's style of banjo storytelling transcends the quaint corniness of tall-tale humor, unearthing a deeper comedy of wounded dignity in the story of the high diver. The driving rhythms of the steel-stringed chords vibrate with the old-fashioned determination displayed by the hero every time he's faced with a new challenge from his competitor. America's heritage of frontier gumption seems to be embedded in every note.

Another aspect of Wade's approach particularly suited to the performance of tall tales is the way he contradicts the tone of what he is saying with the mood of what he is playing. The banjo's wild frailing provides a slow-building counterpoint of outrageous unpredictability to the deadpan delivery of the story's words. When Wade talks about a Louisiana mosquito so big its photograph weighs twelve pounds his voice is calm, but his banjo buzzes like a swarm of giant mosquitoes

ready to attack. The point and counterpoint of Wade's double-barreled presentation dovetails beautifully with the tall tale's demand for a balance between the ordinary and the preposterous. Wade is so skillful at eliciting subtle effects from his banjo that he can even provide the musical equivalent of irony, undercutting the low-keyed tone of his vocal delivery with a whimsical twang that is about as close as a banjo can get to winking its eye.

Another skewed glance at the competitive spirit of the nineteenth-century frontier is found in Wade's tall tale about the hound dog that runs faster than a steam locomotive. With nothing more than his banjo, his boots and a whistle, Wade recreates the atmosphere of excited anticipation that might have accompanied the race between the dog and the "Cannonball Express." The whistle makes the shrieking sound signaling the train's departure from the station. The boots dance the rhythm of the wheels pounding against the track. The banjo strums out the sound of the engine gathering up speed. The combination of sounds conjures up the majestic illusion of a steam-driven train hurtling down an endless expanse of track. The banjo seems to be generating the momentum that keeps the train moving at greater and greater speeds. For the punch line of the story's climactic joke, Wade plays while standing on one foot, imitating the stance of the dog lifting his leg to put out a fire on the train as he runs by.

Wade's banjo does more than musically materialize steamboats, locomotives, and other forms of nineteenth-century machinery. Its music illuminates the inner workings of the characters' hearts and minds. Throughout his wryly funny retelling of Tom Sawyer's adventures whitewashing Aunt Polly's fence, Wade fills in the spaces between Mark Twain's lines with banjo licks that catch the delightfully devious origins of Tom's complex scheme. The banjo music vibrates with the same pungent clarity that characterizes Twain's prose, echoing Tom's glum resignation as he examines "the far-reaching continent of unwhitewashed fence" stretched out before him, and bursting into a cascade of feverish fingerpicking when Tom's restless brain is seized by the idea of maneuvering his friends into doing his work for him. When Tom first suggests to a friend that whitewashing is a privilege rather than a chore, Wade punctuates the crucial pause with suspenseful strumming that explodes into chords of wild joy when the victim falls into the trap, and begs Tom to let him try the whitewashing himself.

"Tom gave up the brush with reluctance in his face, but alacrity in his heart," wrote Twain. Wade delivers the line with reluctance in his voice, but alacrity in his banjo. The music squeals with all the high-pitched pleasure that Tom was barely able to suppress as he "sat on a barrel in the shade close by, dangled his legs, munched his apple, and planned the slaughter of more innocents." The thrill of Tom's internal celebration is heightened by the clog dancing that Wade uses to accompany the furiously happy sound of his unbridled banjo. When Wade lets loose at moments like these, the banjo seems to be the only instrument in the world capable of registering all the eccentric notes of his characters' hearts. Nothing can sing out the traditional American delights of outsmarting a city slicker, clinching a big deal, beating a competitor or putting one over on the public like the breathless delirium of a five-string banjo.

Skillful though he is at evoking upbeat moods with his banjo, Wade does not ignore the darker registers of the instrument's expressive possibilities. In a spooky story about a Tennessee man who lives alone in a cabin, Wade scratches at the banjo's strings and sounding board to make the noise of a monster crawling up the side of the tiny log house. To create the eerie effect of the monster's voice Wade holds the banjo's face up in front of his own and howls into the back of the instrument's resonating chamber. The sound of his voice and the visual stage picture combine to create a haunting effect. The words are wrapped in a ghostly echo, and Wade's head seems to be replaced by a banjo, his body entirely possessed by the instrument that is an extension of his personality all through the performance.

Wade's style of musical storytelling turns the banjo into something resembling a totemic object. Tapping its links to America's past, he communes with it as if it

were a piece of history that could put him in touch with the lives of our collective ancestors by revealing the lost rhythms of their stories, songs and jokes. Playing banjos that were actually constructed before the Civil War, Wade connects the audience to the raw pleasures of lost eras. He brings inert fragments of the past to life with music that evokes a stream of photographic details. Wade's banjo can play the sound of a sunrise, a swamp dog, a howling wind, a dentist extracting a tooth. It also captures the subtler music of jealousy, scheming and irrefutable logic. But even more remarkable than Wade's ability to turn animals, landscapes and emotions into music is his skill at making the cadences of American history resonate from the sounding board of a five-string banjo. The driving momentum of his strumming celebrates a competitive spirit that recalls America's most expansive dreams, while his thoughtful fingerpicking provides a counterpoint of skepticism that highlights the idiosyncratic character of our national foibles. Whether he is telling the story of a frontier hero or an urban confidence man, Wade makes his banjo squeal, shriek, wail, murmur and whistle as if history were a hootenanny and all its ghosts could be resurrected by the frailing of his singing steel strings.

"Fleming's Banjo"

I don't really play this banjo very much. Yet it's the one, it's the very banjo I always wanted. I've always loved its look. I've always loved to hold it—its weight; its feel; its shape. I used to dream about this banjo: how much I wished I could have it; or, if I had this banjo, boy, would I ever play; or if I only had this banjo, well, then I'd be set. Now I have it, it's mine, and I hardly ever play it. I almost never take it out of the case; and it is a good banjo. This was my teacher's banjo, and the first time I ever saw him, this was the banjo he played. It's Fleming's banjo.

His whole name was Fleming Brown, and walking into his classroom and hearing him play for the first time was like standing in the passageway between two moving train cars that are going at ninety miles an hour. The cars are pitching up and down at different rates and there's no handrail to get your balance and it smells like gun metal and diesel grease and the detachable floor made of nonskid stamped-metal plates is clattering in and out. The top half of the doors are open into the night air and the houses and trees and telephone poles are going by, by, by, and with the night noise and the wheel banging and the train bells, it is utterly, everlastingly loud in there. Riding between those train cars or going to a rock concert and hearing the band that played so loud it made the water run out of my ears, I had never heard anything like the way Fleming Brown played the banjo that night.

He took this big old dark worn dog of a banjo; this complication of metal parts and arch top and resonator; this machine of metal and wood that was attached to him; and he made this banjo talk: like a snare drum, like a Cadillac eight, like a harpsichord, like a tear in the throat. He sat there and jockeyed this banjo. He straddled it, all angles and elbows. He sat there with his back straight up, his right hand frailing down the banjo, with his eyes closed and his head turned away to the side. He was pulling apart in two directions. His cowboy boot cracked the floor; everything was cocksure and asymmetrical. He played the banjo like the peal of bells; his fingers pushing, pointing, pulling off the fingerboard.

His music was inexplicable, unimaginable, impossible. How can I account for it? Maybe this way.

Chicago was my home and Fleming's and his teacher's Kentucky-born Doc Hopkins. It is also the home of the Chicago blues. In clubs all over Chicago, you can see and hear the Delta blues remade into a new, amplified music.

My friends and I used to go see a bluesman named Hound Dog Taylor, with his group, the Houserockers. His full name was Theodore Roosevelt Taylor, and he was from Natchez, Mississippi. Like so many other Mississippians, he had moved up to Chicago to the South Side to find work. We'd see him in taverns where he'd play stretched out in a chair. He was a tall, skinny man; a bony long-limbered man. He wore a thin white short-sleeved shirt, tired checkered pants, and on the back of his head, a little fedora hat. His knees would knock back and forth while he played and his head would swing from side to side. He had a four-pickup forest-green solid-body electric guitar that he played with a slide. In his band were two men, a drummer and a guitar player whose white maple fingerboard was streaked black and rutted from use. His hands dug into it, around it, like tentacles, like he could consume it. The drummer kept time while he chewed gum, round and round, always at the same pace. The guitarist had a wild grin, ear to ear and only one or two teeth; and the whole place, all of us, were going nuts. We were making up dances. Mine were the Hieroglyphic and the Rodin. My friend invented the Brush, and another invented the Teapot. We'd be moving so hard, I'd get a blister on my toe inside my sneaker. Hound Dog would pump his legs and wave his head while his steel slide skimmed up the neck. I was in the front row; I just had to listen, couldn't dance anymore, and I looked and I looked again and I counted on my fingers and then I counted back again, and I looked at my hand and I looked at his to check. And there on his left hand, the one with the bottleneck, he had six fingers on that hand. That sixth finger was vestigial; it was little, it didn't do much. But that musician, that spirit, who sang "Rolling and tumbling all night long," that man had eleven fingers. And that's how much sound came out of Fleming's banjo that night.

Like the Delta, like Chicago, like the Appalachian mountains, like Hound Dog Taylor, like this veteran banjo, Fleming's music was tough. One time, my friends and I went to see bluesman Albert King play at a small Northside club. Albert King is a big man, big-shouldered like a football player. He was wearing a gray three-piece suit with sleek wide lapels spread straight out. He played left-handed a rocket-shaped Gibson Flying V electric guitar that was strung backwards. He had a big group too, with backup singers and horn players. After the show, he strode out of there and got on his tour bus. We were parked behind it. That bus took up the width of Wrightwood Avenue and we couldn't pull around it and so we waited while they loaded up. And just as it was getting going, that thing, that refurbished early-sixties Golden Eagle luxuryliner, with his name painted on the side in boxcar letters, that old gray monster that had burned a lot of road miles, that bus ripped out the biggest backfire you ever heard. It was just like the music. Take it or leave it. The night I first saw Fleming, this banjo, like that bus, sounded that rude. It was stark and throaty. Fleming sang with all his force, his insides pouring out. But what made it tough was that you felt that he could back it up; that there was something in reserve; that the music had been

there for a long, long time. You were hearing him, but seeing something else.

Several summers ago, at the Folklife Festival on the Mall in Washington, D.C., I watched a man from the hotel waiter's union set a table. It was a windless, white-sky afternoon. The August air was hot, still and thick; and every thirty seconds the sky was rent by jet noise. I was standing near this tent and there were a couple people over there and I went in, and this waiter, on a little platform with just a table, a place setting and one chair, said he was from a downtown hotel. He was wearing his uniform, with epaulets, high collar, buttoned double-breasted all the way up, like someone in a Sousa marching band. He began: "This is how you serve a formal sit-down breakfast at a banquet. Now say this is a round table with twelve people here. And at each of these settings there are three glasses; one for juice, one for water, and one to remove. Now this napkin, which you fold like this, is kept right here exactly in the center of the plate. Now here's the egg cup, and here's the spoon for the egg. See how these are lined up? You have to have your silverware clean, unspotted and polished. Now this spoon with the serrated edge is for the cantaloupe, or another fruit, what have you. Now after they've done with the juice, you take away the glass, stepping in between them like this. Then you bring your choice of bacon or ham, and here's the butter plate, and you always have a sprig of parsley on the side here to clean the palate with. And you drop two pats of butter on the dish, with a little bit of crushed ice, and then you bring on the breakfast steak. You always fill the coffee cup. Then you wait and then you bring on the strawberries and cream."

And the whole time he said all this, there wasn't any food on the table. It was just a demonstration of the waiter's craft; just a few utensils and some empty plates. But watching that man, I don't think any meal ever tasted so good, nor was any banquet ever such a dignified occasion. It was just like Fleming's songs: there was more to them than what you heard.

This is true too of the Chicago blues. Last year I went to Mississippi to see up close some of the sources of this music. One person I visited was Othar Turner who sings cornfieldhollars—arhoolies—and plays a homemade cane fife. He was having a barbeque in the clearing next to his house, there in Panola County, in the Hill Country of northeastern Mississippi. The party was an annual thing and it went all day and night. Along the sides, for chairs, were old car seats. You could buy a barbeque and a beer. Some men carried pint bottles in their pockets. Kids would laugh and squeal and cars yanked out of the driveway shooting pebbles and dust in every direction. Othar and his three drummers marched loosely around the yard and rocked two steps here, one step back. He'd play an old-time reel or the fragment of a blues tune and the drummers would keep time all around it. Sometimes the rhythm sounded what up North people call the "Hey Bo Diddley" beat. The bass drummer told me that he grew up wanting to play with Othar. They started him on a four-gallon washtub when he was a kid; then graduated him to the side of a panel truck, and finally, when he was good enough, they gave him a regular kettle drum.

I met a man there. He asked me my name. I told him Steve. He said his name was Sam. He said, "See, two S's." He said, "Where you from?" I told him Chicago. So was he, that's where he was born. "What year?" I told him. It was the same for both of us. He said, "See, that's three things right there."

In the field some people were dancing in ragged sneakers and others had hose and high heels on. They called this "jump and kick music." And hours later when I was leaving I went up to Othar and we said good-bye, and then he said, "You tell people about me and I'll tell people about you and that's how we'll get through this thing."

So I remember Othar Turner, and Hound Dog Taylor, and Albert King, and the waiter on the Mall, and the night I first saw Fleming Brown play. I think about them when I hold this banjo. So I don't really need to play this banjo very much.

—*Stephen Wade*

BIG APPLE CIRCUS

"Circus is the original theatre of aspiration."

—PAUL BINDER

The Big Apple Circus is a sawdust spectacle of status and power. Like the city whose nickname it borrows, the one-ring canvas village is full of contradictions. All circuses are hierarchical, but the small scale of the Big Apple's intimate tent makes the class contrasts more immediate. The ringmaster's tuxedo and the trapezist's leotards are ostentatiously opulent, while the comically inadequate garments of the clowns are ill-fitting and frayed. The competition for attention is intense, and the aristocratic ringmaster does not hide his preference for the elite corps of highly skilled acrobats, aerialists and animal trainers. These are the circus equivalent of yuppies, and they enter the ring with the proud assurance of individuals accustomed to a privileged place in the spotlight. The clowns, on the other hand, are the underclass. They slip into the arena behind the ringmaster's back, fully aware that they can be evicted at any moment. Their slapstick routines are designed to subvert the ringmaster's territorial control, and to gain for themselves some of the celebrity status enjoyed by their more highly esteemed colleagues. Like a politician running for reelection the tuxedoed master of ceremonies tries to keep these social deviants out of sight, indignantly resisting their attempts to usurp his power and apologizing to the public for their unseemly acts of desperation. The clowns' interventions in the glittering world of circus overachievement are humbling reminders of the community's imperfections.

One of the comic characters at the lower end of the Big Apple Circus social register is a gray-haired bag lady named Grandma. She hobbles into the ring wearing a shabby red overcoat and kerchief that immediately set her apart from the sleek, sexy gymnasts and equestriennes. The ringmaster tries to usher Grandma politely out of the plush red-carpeted ring, but she insists on performing, and rather than risking an embarrassing scene, he lets her stay, humoring her with the opportunity to sing a song. The seemingly feeble old woman, actually played by a man, shocks the audience with a fiercely sexual lip-synced rendition of rhythm-and-blues. She shakes her hips provocatively and mouths strong

JEFF GORDON
(GORDOON), MICHAEL
CHRISTENSEN
(MR. STUBBS) AND
BARRY LUBIN
(GRANDMA).

phrases like "I'm staying! I'm staying!" and "You're gonna love me!" Eventually the ringmaster orders his stage manager to escort Grandma out of the ring. The scene is reminiscent of a maître d' ordering a security guard to remove an undesirable street person from a fancy restaurant. The serious circus performers are like the regular customers, treated with a respect befitting their European pedigrees and international renown. Grandma's insistent demand for equal time is a spunky comic challenge to the exclusivity of their elite domain.

Barry Lubin, who originated the character of Grandma, is one of a trio of clowns who worked together at the Big Apple Circus from 1983 to 1987. The other two are Michael Christensen and Geff Gordon, who continued performing with the show after Lubin's departure in '87. Although the Big Apple Circus has employed a number of talented clowns since its founding in 1977, the trio of Lubin, Christensen and Gordon created an exciting style of ensemble clowning that is rare in modern American circuses. Their comedy was deftly integrated into the context of the circus acts that surrounded them. The clowns humanized the virtuosity of their fellow performers with routines rooted in the fears and desires of ordinary people. They provided an emotional link between the audience and the seemingly superhuman circus artists whose accomplishments appear to elevate them beyond the realm of human feeling. Grandma's yearning for dignity is an effective counterpoint to the regal acrobatics of the female superstars. The wildly childish joy of Geff Gordon's clown, an irrepressible and wacky character named Gordoon, is the antithesis of the cool detachment displayed by the macho circus strongmen around him. Michael Christensen plays the role of a tramp clown named Mr. Stubbs. His frustrated dreams and tattered tailcoat make him look like the impoverished alter ego of the eminently successful and elegantly attired ringmaster.

In European circuses the ringmaster is traditionally a foil for the clowns. At the Big Apple Circus the rivalry is Americanized as a battle between the haves and the have-nots. The clowns reappear throughout the show like unwanted homeless

GRANDMA, GORDOON
AND MR. STUBBS WITH
RINGMASTER PAUL
BINDER.

vagabonds. The ringmaster who keeps trying to evict them is played by Paul Binder, the circus's managing director and a Columbia University MBA. The clowns are always in a state of comic insurrection against the ringmaster's authority. He is the landlord of the ring, a tyrant of common sense and public decorum who sees it as his duty to suppress the clowns' irrational impulses.

When Mr. Stubbs interrupts the flow of the circus with a nonsensical juggling routine, the ringmaster tries to stop him by confiscating one of his balls. Stubbs instantly inserts another ball into his juggling pattern. The ringmaster grabs another, and another, and eventually begins juggling three balls himself to prevent Stubbs from continuing with his act of insubordination. But the balls seem to be flying in and out of the ringmaster's hands against his will, as if the clown's irrepressible sense of anarchy were a contagious disease that had infected the ringmaster without his realizing it. In an attempt to handle his dilemma with dignity, the ringmaster juggles in an orderly manner, but Stubbs disrupts him again by replacing balls with strangely shaped objects that are more difficult to control. When the ringmaster finds himself juggling a club with two balls, he protests, "Wait, that's an unlike object!" Stubbs responds by slipping another club into the ringmaster's pattern, substituting an adjective for a verb while he's at it. "How do you unlike that?" the clown quips, wreaking havoc with syntax and the ringmaster's nerves simultaneously.

Christensen and Binder first began working together as members of the San Francisco Mime Troupe in the early seventies. That company's style of physical satire accustomed them to making their points through the metaphor of juggling. In a 1973 Mime Troupe play entitled *Frozen Wages* Binder, Christensen and other members of the troupe expressed the effects of factory layoffs and increased production demands with a group juggling routine. Workers passed clubs back and forth to represent their work on the line. Each time one of them got laid off, fewer workers were forced to pass more clubs at swifter velocities. The unfair

GORDOON, GRANDMA AND
THE RINGMASTER.

burden was made vivid by the quickened rhythms and spinning trajectories of the juggling clubs.

Other clowns in the circus do not share Christensen's onstage rapport with Binder, but they too are experts in expressing their irreverence in bursts of highly skilled physical action. When Gordoon manages to slip by the ringmaster and infiltrate the ring long enough to balance on a giant sphere, he leaps off the globe with a back flip that physicalizes his exuberant sense of triumph over authority. The celebratory effect of the moment is strengthened by Gordoon's releasing a handful of colored confetti into the air as he jumps. His ecstasy is short-lived, however, because he promptly begins to worry that the ringmaster will punish him for dirtying the ring with confetti.

Gordoon fetches an air-blowing machine to sweep away the confetti, but ends up having so much fun playing with it that he forgets all about cleaning. When the ringmaster returns he finds the clown balancing a balloon globe on the airstream of the blow-gun. Gordoon's manipulations of the globe clownishly echo Chaplin's famous dance in *The Great Dictator*, but instead of keeping the world at his fingertips as Chaplin's Hitler did, Gordoon keeps the world adroitly balanced under the seat of his pants. This, of course, is unacceptable to the ringmaster, who confiscates the globe and leaves the ring. Left alone in search of another plaything, the resourceful clown pulls a roll of toilet paper out of a secret compartment in the ring curb. He unfurls the tissue in the wind of the blowing machine, and dances gleefully underneath the cascades of white paper.

At another point in the show Gordoon expresses his liberation from social restraint by literally flying through the air. Having witnessed one of the aerial acts, he begins to flap his arms. At first nothing happens, but then he takes a running start, waves his arms again, and rises a few feet off the ground. His levitation is actually achieved by a cable attached to a harness under the clown's clothes, but he seems oblivious to the contraption, convinced that his flapping arms have the power to send him skyward. With Grandma's encouragement

GORDOON, OAF, FISH (JOHN LEPIARZ) AND MR. STUBBS.

Gordoon flails his way wildly back and forth across the ring, gaining altitude each time he reaches the opposite ring curb, until he is sailing blissfully over the upturned heads of the laughing crowd.

Not until he finds himself at the top of the blue-and-red canvas tent does Gordoon take a moment to look down at the faces below him. When he notices how far down they are, he is terrified. Up until then the flying clown had soared through the air with his limbs extended like some absurd emblem of wingless freedom. But the minute he considers the possibility of falling, his body is instantly transformed into the personification of panic. Clinging to the top of the center pole that supports the tent, Gordoon shrinks into a quivering mass of human fear. His body is an emotional barometer, amplifying his condition so powerfully that everyone in the tent empathizes with his predicament.

"Whatever you do, don't panic," urges the ringmaster over the microphone. A shriek of terror is the clown's immediate response. By the time Gordoon slides down from the top of the tent in what seems a miraculous escape, the clown has brought the audience a little closer to the human impulses that make the circus tick. The triple somersaults of the trapeze artists are to be admired from afar, but the clown who tries and fails to fly tells a story that's close enough to touch.

Earlier in the circus Grandma also exhibits clownish desires to fly, but her aspirations are more complex than Gordoon's. Grandma's fantasies are inspired by the aerial ballet of the beautiful bikini-clad Dolly Jacobs. Grandma doesn't just want to fly. She wants to be sexy too. The incongruity between her wishes and her age sets up a series of comic moments that mock the circus stereotypes of feminine beauty.

Dolly Jacobs' extraordinary athletic abilities are complemented by a strong body endowed with all the typically accepted attributes of female desirability. Her aerial act is lithe and sensuous. The program note that accompanies her photograph quotes a passage from Thomas Mann: "She was a solemn angel of daring with parted lips and dilated nostrils, that is what she was, an unapproachable

Amazon of the realms of space beneath the canvas, high above the crowd, whose lust for her was transformed into awe."

Grandma, of course, is everything that Dolly Jacobs is not. The gray-haired matron who inspires laughter could almost be a photographic negative of the dark-haired Amazon who inspires awe. Jacobs' body is shapely, smooth and limber. Grandma walks stiffly in a baggy red overcoat. Jacobs' balletic grace is matched by Grandma's staccato clumsiness. But Grandma is determined to shatter society's notions of permissible behavior for the elderly. She wants to fly through the air. She wants to be desired. She wants to make a grand exit that leaves the crowd hungry for more. So she does. And in the process she challenges the ringmaster's conservative vision of what is acceptable in the circus.

First, Grandma interrupts the show. When the ringmaster orders her to find a seat and behave herself, she begins flirting with a gentleman in the audience and sits on his lap. She expresses her admiration for Dolly Jacobs, but as she climbs on and off the ring curb her tiny deliberate steps suggest that she can never imitate her idol. "You can't swing on the trapeze without a catcher," counsels the ringmaster. He is referring to the acrobat who hangs upside down to catch the aerialist flying from one trapeze to another, but Grandma produces a different kind of catcher. She whistles and Gordoon appears in a baseball uniform with a catcher's mitt, and escorts Grandma to the trapeze.

Grandma's slapstick trapeze act is a multileveled parody of Jacobs' erotic aerial ballet. The clown is twice removed from youthful femininity, but she proves that she too has the right and the power to seduce the audience's attention with airborne acrobatics of her own. She demands the audience's applause and the ringmaster's praise. She also insists on being escorted out of the ring on the arms of two men, just as Jacobs was. Grandma's trapeze act mocks Jacobs' by being intentionally inferior to it; Grandma's exit mocks Jacobs' by surpassing it in flair and bravado.

When the ringmaster begins to lead Grandma out of the ring, she wiggles her

DOLLY JACOBS.

bottom and refuses to be led docilely away. The diminutive old lady drags the stage manager to the ground, turns to the audience and breaks into another song. Again the music is recorded and Grandma is only lip-syncing, but the gyrations of her body make it clear that she means what she's singing. The song is "Respect" by Aretha Franklin, and respect is obviously what Grandma has been asking for all along. She soulfully shimmies her way through the lyrics until she gets it.

Grandma's fierce independence encourages us to reexamine Jacobs' stereotypical femininity, especially as it is communicated in the aerialist's exit. After completing an astonishing series of midair acrobatic feats, Jacobs comes down to the ground and is helped into her high-heeled shoes by her two male escorts, as if a woman who can do somersaults in the air needs help to put on her shoes. Once she is down on the ringmaster's turf she accepts the role of female subservience and allows the men to lead her out of the limelight. Grandma, however, calls attention to the paradox by flattening one of her escorts and throwing them both out of the ring, while she belts out a musical command for respect. Jacobs is content to win respect for her acrobatics in the air, but Grandma wants hers down on the ground where it counts.

In the course of challenging the ringmaster and the stereotypes he embraces, the clowns often create episodes of surreal visual poetry. In a 1984 routine Mr. Stubbs entered the ring with a butterfly net and a peanut-butter-and-jelly sandwich. He is hunting butterflies, and is convinced that they can't resist peanut butter. The ringmaster, playing the cruel voice of reason, informs the clown that there are no butterflies in the circus. Told to give up his absurd search, he falls into a dejected sleep in the center of the ring. The lights dim, the band plays softly, and the clown is visited by the kind of butterflies that could exist only in the mind of a clown. Winged ballerinas dance around his sleeping form. A tiny dog with wings waddles to his side. Grandma hovers over his head like an aging angel, swooping down to give him a kiss. There are also appearances by winged hillbillies and butterfly aerialists, but the climax of the scene comes when Mr. Stubbs wakes to find an elephant with wings standing over him. Delighted to discover that the butterfly elephant does indeed like peanut-butter-and-jelly sandwiches, he rides the fantastical creature out of the ring, overjoyed to have proven the ringmaster wrong. The poetic dream logic of the clown triumphs over the mundane reasoning of authority, and Mr. Stubbs' victory chariot is a pachyderm with plastic wings.

Despite their poetic victories, the clowns never escape their roles as beleaguered underdogs in the circus world of overachievers. Their parodies of the other performers emphasize their inferior status in comic terms. After an animal trainer dressed as the lord of the jungle proves he can tame an elephant, a leopard and a sexy female assistant with equal ease, Mr. Stubbs enters in the rags of a Bowery bum and proves himself incapable of taming even a lowly flea. In 1984 the clowns created a mock Olympics. Surrounded by circus performers of extraordinary physical prowess, the clowns exhibited their skills in ice dancing by wiggling their hips with ice cubes in their pants. The clown games were inaugurated with the lighting of the Olympic torch, a ceremony performed in tattered underwear by a breathless Mr. Stubbs with a Bic lighter.

The clowns' vision of themselves as perpetual losers in America's competitive society came through clearly in their 1985 parody of *Wheel of Fortune*. It begins with Mr. Stubbs interrupting the ringmaster by repeatedly chanting the phrase "Big money. Big money." The clown claims to be the host of a game show called *Wheel of Misfortune*. Vanna White's role as the young and beautiful hostess is filled by Grandma, who is introduced as "a priceless antique" with a retail value of "about four dollars." The reigning champion of the show is Gordoon, billed as "Mr. Misfortune himself," who trips and falls on his face as he enters the ring to compete in a new round. The game is clearly rigged so that neither the clown nor his opponent, an audience volunteer, can win anything of value. When the volunteer is promised a brand-new car, crashing sounds are heard behind the curtain, and a battered tire rolls out as the only surviving remnant of her prize. "How misfortunate," laments Mr. Stubbs, whose words of commiseration become the recurring motif of the contest. Gordoon is equally unlucky, exchanging a prize worth millions for a bucket of water that is poured on his head. Mr. Stubbs responds to Gordoon's disappointment by leading the audience in the now-familiar chorus of hollow consolation: "How misfortunate."

The spectators at the Big Apple Circus are encouraged to identify with the clowns. The grease-painted losers suffer the same indignities that plague the average person who falls behind in the American race for wealth, fame and success. Surrounded by stereotypes of sexy women, macho men and aristocratic power brokers, they scurry to find a niche for themselves between the star turns of the main attractions. Unable to fit the image of youthful strength and perfection being applauded all around them, the clowns invent their own modest dreams of fulfillment. Content with a wreath of toilet paper, a pair of plastic wings, a chance to sing the blues, the Big Apple clowns are model survivors in a one-ring community of unequal opportunities.

THE FLYING KARAMAZOV BROTHERS

"Juggling is a way of integrating things. It's like a laser. A laser takes

incoherent light, all kinds of different wavelengths, and focuses it. The

audience gives us all this unfocused energy, and we just reflect it back

to them in a more organized way. So they have the sense

of seeing these guys who are just like them."

—RANDY NELSON

The Flying Karamazov Brothers take fragmented bits of American miscellany and juggle them into patchwork symphonies of visual jazz. They hum songs from the fifties, shout slogans from the sixties, act out movie scenes from the seventies, and throw everyday objects from the eighties around the stage without losing a beat. Airborne ukeleles, frying pans and baseball bats are juxtaposed against random references to Errol Flynn, Star Wars and Dwight D. Eisenhower. The percussive rhythms of the throws and catches give the performance its driving momentum and the verbal non sequiturs provide the quirky melodies. A typical Karamazov show is a surrealistic jam session pulsing with comic improvisations on the icons of American culture.

The musical dimension of the Karamazov act is rooted in the group's ability to change the time signature of their performance by varying the spin on the objects being juggled. They have discovered that tossing a club so that it is caught after a single spin in the air is the equivalent of an eighth note. A double spin results in a three-eighth note, and a half note can be achieved with a high, slow variation on a single spin. This degree of analysis enables them to play Bach on a xylophone while juggling between the notes, at the same time that it provides a technical basis for their improvisational instincts. On a good night they can throw, bounce, spin and bang their juggling clubs with the superheated abandon of a big band in full swing.

The percussive rhythms of a Karamazov performance are accentuated by the well-timed jokes, puns, sight gags and audience-participation events that are layered into the jazzlike structure of the juggling. The so-called Brothers (none of them are related) speak in short silly phrases that echo the crisp syncopated patterns of their juggling routines. Introducing the odd array of objects they choose to juggle, the Karamazovs take turns poking fun at themselves, the audience and the eccentricities of American society. They toss their words deftly between flying torches, meat cleavers, apples and swords. No concept is drawn out too long or explained with excessive detail. One of them claims to be a master

AVNER THE ECCENTRIC,
SAM WILLIAMS, PAUL
MAGID, RANDY NELSON
AND JEFF RAZ
CONFRONT A PIE
THROWER IN THE
LINCOLN CENTER
VERSION OF COMEDY OF
ERRORS.

of "oralgamy," the ancient Asian art of folding words. This is an appropriate term to describe the troupe's habit of honing down language into bite-sized vaudevillian nuggets.

The Karamazovs' most complex exhibition of their improvisational jazz technique is a collage of freeform juggling patterns that spark extemporaneous verbal commentary. When the five jugglers start passing their fifteen clubs in higher and higher arcs, a frightening logjam over their heads seems to increase significantly the probability of midair collisions. The situation inspires one of them to make a quick pun about "air traffic control" at the local airport. When a missed catch actually does set off a chain reaction of dropped clubs, another Brother yells "Meltdown!" The reference to Three Mile Island leads still another to chime in: "We're having an event." The dropping of the clubs does not destroy the percussive beat of the ensemble. They simply use the musical gaps created by mistakes to provoke improvisational changes. Risk is incorporated into the show as an element of rhythmic variation.

Free associations move the group from nuclear accidents to the Vietnam War, as four members of the group begin advancing on the point man receiving their passes. Playing on the fact that the spinning clubs resemble the whirling blades of army helicopters, they all begin humming Wagner's "Ride of the Valkyries," creating the jugglers' equivalent of *Apocalypse Now*. Later, when a Brother begins to systematically remove clubs from the pattern, a complaint is registered in tones of mock alarm: "What is this, some kind of weird trickle-down theory?" The quip links Ronald Reagan's economic theories to a juggling image that suggests diminished opportunities for all.

Juggling provides the Flying Karamazov Brothers with an abundance of metaphors that enable them to filter high art and politics through the fractured lens of popular culture. The mirror game begins with their name, which suggests a Dostoyevsky novel transformed into a circus act. Displaying pseudo-Russian costumes and stereotypical Russian names, the Brothers juggle sickles and make

HOWARD PETTERSON, TIMOTHY FURST, PAUL MAGID, SAM WILLIAMS AND RANDY NELSON.

puns on the Russian word *nyet,* but their show has nothing to do with the homeland of Dostoyevsky's characters. The name of the troupe is just a springboard to irreverence. It forewarns the audience that the American egalitarianism of the Karamazovs will reduce anything in their path to the common denominator of comic anarchy.

The troupe's aesthetic stance can be traced back to its members' years as students and street performers in the San Francisco Bay area. Their shoulder-length hair and beards are left over from the antiestablishment mood of the early seventies. Most of the Brothers went to the University of California at Santa Cruz, where the student activists espoused the same kind of collective values emphasized by the collaborative nature of group juggling. Defying gravity in a juggling act could be seen as a parallel to defying authority in an antiwar demonstration. To a generation of idealists who believed that radical political change and social justice were achievable goals, the performance of outlandish feats of juggling was a way of affirming that anything is possible.

The Karamazov show entitled *Juggle and Hyde* centers around their continuing efforts to pull off an impossible stunt. Inventing more and more complex tasks for themselves, the troupe satirizes their search for perfection as they engage in it, asking "Why would somebody want to become the best in the world doing something that most people don't even know exists?" The response they give themselves is framed in a potpourri of American cliches from television, film and the theatre about dreaming the impossible dream, climbing every mountain, and exploring where no man has gone before. Each challenge they present themselves is dismissed as too easy, as they convince themselves that they have to try something bigger and better. "It's the American way," they proclaim. The tricks are punctuated with disconnected comic one-liners about Little Red Riding Hood, the Addams Family, performance art, Japanese haiku, and "our acting President" until the end of the show, when they finally devise a geometrically tortuous pattern of passing different-colored clubs to one another that they declare to be

THE THREE
MOSCOWTEERS.

certifiably impossible. After failing a few times, they manage to make it work, and the results are exhilarating. The syncopated sounds of the catches are rhythmically satisfying to the ear, and the dizzying flight of the clubs is mesmerizing to the eye. But just when they seem to have reached perfection, a wall of cardboard boxes topples over on them, revealing them once again as flawed mortals who have encountered a set of obstacles that puts them in their place.

The Karamazovs' ongoing struggles with the impossible take place in a context saturated with the iconography of America's melting pot. In their first Broadway success, *Juggling and Cheap Theatrics*, one of the running gags was the accumulation of a pile of disparate objects that were to be juggled together at the end of the show. Each addition to the bizarre collection was introduced with corny jokes and campy songs that made reference to everything from Hamlet to Popeye. There were Latin chants, French catch phrases, and the ritual sacrifice of a Big Mac. In the end the objects to be juggled included a meat cleaver, a skillet, a torch, an egg, a pair of handcuffs, a ukelele and a bottle of California champagne. The Brothers threw them all into the air and ended up chopping the eggs with the meat cleaver, cooking them in the skillet by the heat of the torch, and celebrating the meal with a chord on the ukelele, while two Brothers in handcuffs offered a champagne toast to the success of the endeavor. All of this happened in a matter of seconds, enabling the Karamazovs to satisfy their audience's craving for fast food, cheap wine and dinner theatre all at the same time.

Despite the difficulty of their antics, the Karamazovs try to avoid setting themselves apart from their public. They maintain a direct relationship with the spectators by calling attention to their mistakes, inviting volunteers onto the stage, and explaining the techniques of what they are doing as they perform. And when they disagree about what constitutes the essence of their work, they let the audience in on the argument. At one point in *Juggling and Cheap Theatrics* three of the Brothers debate the true nature of juggling. Ivan claims that juggling is a science. Smerdyakov maintains that juggling is only a trick. Dimitri asserts that

THE GOODMAN THEATRE PRODUCTION OF <u>COMEDY OF ERRORS</u>. 65

juggling is an art. This might seem rather an abstract debate to insert into a fast-moving variety show, but the Karamazovs illustrate the subtleties of their arguments with feats of juggling that support their points of view.

Not content with the success of their juggling variety shows, the Karamazovs often experiment with ways of integrating their physical skills into dramatic texts with linear plots. The most challenging of these experiments to date were the Karamazov versions of Stravinsky's *L'Histoire du Soldat* and Shakespeare's *Comedy of Errors*. Neither of the productions was entirely successful, but they did reveal the troupe's skill at transforming juggling into a uniquely American form of fragmented visual music.

L'Histoire du Soldat was presented by the Karamazovs at the Brooklyn Academy of Music's 1986 Next Wave Festival. The troupe collaborated with an eclectic jazz ensemble known as the Kamikaze Ground Crew, and with a collection of actors who knew how to tap dance, juggle, turn back flips and eat fire. Paul Magid (Dimitri) and playwright Len Jenkin rewrote the original libretto, setting the piece in post-Vietnam America.

Stravinsky's hero is a soldier who trades his violin to the devil for wealth and power. The Karamazov hero is a Vietnam vet who sells his juggling balls to the devil in exchange for a taste of the American dream. Sam Williams (Smerdyakov) plays the lead role of Joe King, the common man who wants to be rich. Paul Magid is the devil who invites Joe to his condo, where he is promised enough money to merit an appearance on *Lifestyles of the Rich and Famous*. The devil's assistant is named Vanna, and has the vapid sexuality of the television game-show hostess. The text satirizes America's blind consumerism with a cornucopia of jokes about chain stores, shopping malls, burger joints and suburbia, but the production has long dry stretches in which the performers' physical skills are not employed. What makes the popular-culture references work in the Karamazov variety shows is the skill with which they are incorporated into the rhythms of the juggling and physical comedy. In *L'Histoire du Soldat* the satire is conceptualized with intelligence and integrity, but the topical humor is not dramatic enough to stand on its own.

The piece comes to life when music, juggling and story intersect. Stravinsky's recurring violin solo is accompanied by a three-ball juggling routine that captures all the playful quirkiness of the music. Sam Williams as Joe King tosses the balls under his legs and rolls them off the bald spot on his head. On the staccato notes he tosses the balls in a low quick juggling rhythm, shifting to long, high-arcing throws when the music slows down. In the original version, the soldier loses his soul when he loses his violin. Williams makes the loss of his juggling balls equally devastating by matching their movements so delicately to the music.

Another moment when the juggling coalesces perfectly with the music and the story comes when Joe meets the princess of the North and wins her hand in marriage by waking her from a icy sleep. Williams expresses the soft seductive quality of their first encounter by juggling white scarves. They float as teasingly as the lilting notes of Stravinsky's score, and the princess responds by tossing three of her own scarves playfully into the air. They steal and pass the billowing pieces of cloth in the juggling equivalent of prenuptial foreplay, and by the time the music ends they are juggling pillows.

The Karamazovs are also central figures in the highly physicalized version of *Comedy of Errors* produced by Greg Mosher at the Goodman Theatre in Chicago and then at Lincoln Center in New York. Ephesus, the scene of the play's action, is presented as a gathering place for seasoned vaudevillians, where everybody knows how to juggle and tell a good joke. Although the Karamazovs are less than poetic in their execution of Shakespeare's language, the premise did create great opportunities for the kind of multicultural variety show at which the troupe excels. Shakespeare is Americanized with references to Jackie Gleason, Oliver North, *Gone with the Wind*, *Sesame Street*, Burma Shave and Madonna's "Material Girl." The Kamikaze Ground Crew band provides steamy jazz while clothed in such garments as a Turkish fez, Scottish kilts, a French beret, Indian turbans and Mickey Mouse ears.

Some critics were concerned at the loss of the play's moral center, but the vaudevillian approach gives the production a muscularity that American actors rarely achieve in Shakespearean comedy. The threat of death that hangs over the play's farcical action is embodied by the genuine risk-taking of aerial trapeze artist Wendy Parkman, on loan from the Pickle Family Circus. Former baton-twirling champion Sophie Hayden expresses Adriana's jealous rage with the wild spinning of a sword, reflecting the power of her words in the glistening fury of her sharpened blade. Under the direction of Robert Woodruff (who also staged *L'Histoire du Soldat*) the energy of the physical acting gives needed velocity and momentum to a play that is acknowledged to be one of Shakespeare's slightest.

The Karamazov attempts to Americanize European classics are fascinating experiments in the blending of text and spectacle, but the group's most representative work is the material they write for themselves. Shows like *Juggling and Cheap Theatrics* and *Juggle and Hyde* may lack the refinement of Shakespeare and Stravinsky, but they capture the pulse of America's polyglot culture in the crude energy of the idiomatic form the Karamazovs have invented for themselves. Their fragmented collage of juggling and one-liners has the rhythmic drive of an urban street game, where the onlookers are invited to participate by shouting out their opinion or throwing things into the action.

"The Gamble" is a good example of the Karamazov technique in all its raucous eloquence. A trademark piece that appears in all their stage shows, "The Gamble" is a challenge to the audience in which the Karamazovs declare their willingness to juggle anything the spectators bring onto the stage. The Brothers present Ivan Karamazov as their champion who will get a standing ovation if he succeeds in juggling the audience's offerings, and a pie in the face if he fails. The public comes prepared for the wager. They bombard the stage with bowling balls, Slinky toys, coffee grounds, phone books and other seemingly unjuggleable items. The

mountain of paraphernalia could serve as a time capsule of contemporary American tastes, and the Karamazovs' improvised responses to each object heighten the impression that they are attempting to juggle the pieces of a national patchwork quilt.

A bottle of French's mustard is hailed as an ingredient for American gourmet cooking. "Erin Go Braless" is the punning response to a St. Patrick's Day cake. At the sight of a baseball bat the troupe breaks into the spontaneous reenactment of a Stan Musial home run. The three most difficult objects to juggle are selected by an audience voice vote. One of the Brothers turns himself into a human applause meter to measure the volume of their cheers. Another informs the audience of the rules of the game. "Here's the deal," he begins, as he explains the "fine print" in their verbal contract that gives the champion the right to modify the objects three times before he gets the pie in the face. "That's democracy for you," sums up another when the act nears its inevitable climax of a standing ovation for the champ.

The Flying Karamazov Brothers offer their audiences a performance that combines the elements of game show, amateur hour, sporting event, gambling casino, business deal and election campaign. They have created a series of anarchic spectacles in which five ordinary guys struggle to cope with overwhelming numbers of material objects that fly at them from all directions. Some of the items have sharp edges, some are on fire, and some are ridiculous. But no matter what gets thrown at them, the Karamazovs manage to keep everything up in the air. They offer a reassuring entertainment for the average overwrought American who is bombarded by an overload of stressful demands. Though their world seems to be falling apart around them, the Flying Karamazov Brothers never panic. They just pick up the pieces, make a few jokes, and juggle the chaos of consumerism into a polyphonic display of airborne American jazz.

From *Juggling and Cheap Theatrics*

IVAN: We've seen how the rhythm of throws and catches makes juggling a musical system. If we add to that system the possibility of passing the juggling instruments from one musician to another, then our level of difficulty increases linearly with respect—

SMERDY: Wait a minute, wait a minute! Stop the music!

IVAN: What's the matter Smerdyakov?

SMERDY: You're making this far too complicated Ivan. These are everyday lay people. Well maybe every other day. And they're not accustomed to your technical jargon. Explain it to them in a simpler way.

IVAN: Oh sure I'll try. Let's see . . . . If we then add to the system the possibility of bouncing the juggling subjects while simultaneously passing them, then our level of difficulty increases not only linearly, but exponentially with respect to a dihedral matrix which—

SMERDY: WHOA! WHOA! Hold your horses there big fella. Look, juggling is music and music is juggling, so what? Look ladies and gentlemen, juggling music looks and sounds real purty, and when you add music-making and hitting stuff at the same time it can get even purtier.

IVAN: Smerdyakov, you're such a cretin.

SMERDY: No, I'm from Seattle.

DMITRI: Please, please stop both of you. Now look, juggling is not just a mathematical sequence, nor is it a trick which can be easily explained away. Why, it's an art *(Produces rose and licks petals)* and therefore must be experienced.

Smerdy bites off the rose and spits it on the ground.

SMERDY: Art schmart! All this art fooforall is just a bunch of hooey! It's just a juggling trick.

IVAN: It's not just a trick, it's a mathematical progression of musical beats.

DMITRI: It's an Art!

SMERDY: It's a Trick!

IVAN: It's a Science!

DMITRI: You insensitive boors!

IVAN: You ignorant plebian louts!

SMERDY: You, you beanpockets!

Ivan and Dmitri slam Smerdy with gloves as if to challenge him to a duel.

DMITRI: Imagine saying beanpockets.

Smerdy and Ivan slam Dmitri with gloves.

IVAN: You'll never catch me saying beanpockets. *(He takes gloves and slaps himself)*

ALL: Choose your weapons!

IVAN: South Korean voting machines!

DMITRI: *Roget's Thesaurus* at twenty paces!

SMERDY: Bungee cords!

IVAN: Excellent. Doctor?

Fyodor enters with three swords under his arm. All three grab swords and engage in a slapstick swordfight.

DMITRI: It's an Art.

IVAN: It's a Science.

SMERDY: *(Removes sword from under skewered arm)*: It's a trick. Wait! I've got a rubber rat here and I'm not afraid to use it! *(Brandishes rat)*

DMITRI: You can't fool me with that rubber novelty.

SMERDY: Oh yeah? Kill, Herbert!

Rat attacks Dmitri's neck, Dmitri stabs rat.

SMERDY: No Herbert, Herbert, speak to me Herbert! (*Tries mouth-to-mouth resuscitation, then turns to Dmitri*) He's dead! You dirty brother, you killed my rat! You're a bad person.

IVAN: You have no soul.

SMERDY: You're a heel.

IVAN: You're effete.

SMERDY AND IVAN: And you gotta big nose.

DMITRI: Big nose my foot! You might have insulted me more artistically. For instance, you could have quoted Cyrano and said, ". . . a peninsula." Any last requests?

SMERDY: How about *Hamlet* Act 3 Scene 4?

DMITRI: Something classical. "How now a rat dies for a ducat."

IVAN AND SMERDY: Stabs curtain.

DMITRI: Oh yes, stage directions, very important.

Dmitri stabs center curtain, Alyosha and Fyodor fall out of the two side curtains.

IVAN: It's a Science!

DMITRI: Garcon!

Candelabra appears from between curtains, Dmitri knocks off the top half of the candles.

DIMITRI: It's an Art.

Polite applause.

IVAN (*Grabs Smerdy's sword and points it at him*): Where are your tricks now, little man?

Smerdy pulls fake rabbit out of his hat.

DMITRI: I get it, tricks and art they're the same things.

IVAN (*Sneers*): Tricks, art, for kids.

DMITRI: Au contraire monsieur, they're all three in a word, it's jugglery.

IVAN (*While juggling all three swords*): I get it, one and one and one is three.

DMITRI: All for one!

SMERDY: And three for a dollar!

—*The Flying Karamazov Brothers*

WENDY PARKMAN, PAUL MAGID, RANDY NELSON AND LAUREL CRONIN IN THE GOODMAN THEATRE'S COMEDY OF ERRORS.

Le Cirque du Soleil

"This is not a circus of the future. It's a circus of the present. It only seems like the future, because all the other circuses are in the past."

—DENIS LACOMBE

There are no calliopes or ringmasters in Le Cirque du Soleil. Old-fashioned circus music has been replaced by the pulsing rhythms of electronic synthesizers. The acrobats and aerialists follow one another into the ring without pause for formal introductions. They appear and disappear like shimmering images in an ever-shifting video montage. The performances are fast and flashy. Sharp gestures of transition serve as quick cuts into each new series of body configurations. Two trapezists hang in the air by their ankles, their necks, their calves. Bicyclists ride on their heads, their backs, their hands. The velocity with which the visual patterns change is dizzying, as if they all have trained their muscles to function as speed-efficient editing machines.

In the high-tech sheen of Cirque du Soleil, most of the clowns are reduced to playing the role of remote-control channel changers. They materialize between the acts and vanish in the glare of flashing colored lights. As the teeterboard jumping act sets up its equipment, a clown in prison stripes slides down a pole with a ball and chain on his leg. His mock escape is accompanied by a computerized light show and a bass line on the synthesizer that sounds like the blips in a video game. The staccato sounds and images blur smoothly into the bouncing gymnastics of the teeterboard artists. Sporting bowler hats and suitcases, the comic acrobats leap, flip and fly with the absurd fervor of energetic travelers on a ten-day package tour.

The sophisticated juxtaposition of lights, music, acrobats and clowns gives Cirque du Soleil the feel of a slickly produced music video. The imagery is arresting. The technical wizardry is impressive. The action flows from moment to moment with a synthetic smoothness that eliminates the necessity for meaning, emotion or narrative continuity. There is a thread of narrative running through the circus, but it is sustained primarily by visual connections that are satisfying to the senses, but ultimately hollow. Like the electronic entertainment it emulates so effectively, Cirque du Soleil manufactures the illusion of significance without its substance.

The circus's pretensions are established in the opening moments when a parade of clownish masked figures appear in a mist. Astonished to find themselves in a circus tent, they eventually are transformed into acrobats and wire-walkers. Enveloped in a fog of dry ice and dim lights, these bumbling clowns are clearly meant to be stand-ins for the audience. Like us they are ordinary mortals about to be enchanted by the magic of the circus.

One of the principal agents of this transformation is a silent sinuous master of ceremonies in white face and sequins who writhes acrobatically along with almost every act in the show. He is another of the channel-changing clowns, presiding over the circus transitions with a sinister decadence that suggests he is a descendant of Joel Grey's character in *Cabaret*. When one of the female masked figures runs timidly away from the slack rope, he covers her with a parasol and instantly metamorphoses her into a glamorous wire-walker in a sleek blue bodysuit. The moment suggests that the electronic magic of Cirque du Soleil can transform even the most ordinary individual into a virtuoso performer. Hard work, practice and sweat are eliminated by the wonders of quick-changing remote control.

Traditionally circus clowns use the ringmaster as their foil. Their comic ingenuity becomes a tool of rebellion against his aristocratic authority. In Cirque du Soleil the pace of the show is dictated not by a lordly figure in top hat and tails, but by the more insidious tyranny of the technology behind the synthesizers and lighting effects. Most of the clowns seem to be in a subservient rather than rebellious relationship to the technological ringmaster of Cirque du Soleil. A clown impersonating a security guard walks through the audience with a walkie-talkie clutched to his chest, spitting Ping-Pong balls at the audience with the eerie accuracy of an automated crowd-control device. A comic juggler flips his balls crisply through the air to the accompaniment of computerized traffic sounds. A clown karate expert prepares to smash a brick with slow-motion gestures that recall the special effects in a kung fu movie.

While most of the comic performers succumb limply to the high-tech tyranny of Cirque du Soleil, one clown battles fiercely to maintain his identity. His name is Denis Lacombe, and his relationship to the technological aesthetics dominating the circus is complex and ambiguous. At first glance he seems to be more blatantly oppressed by machinery than any other figure in the circus, but paradoxically he ends up subverting the forces of technology by allowing them to swallow him up. While his colleagues seem to disappear into their fast-moving surroundings, Denis Lacombe stands out as an eccentric figure of beleaguered humanity. He transcends the blandness of his electronic environment by satirizing the absurdity of man's enslavement to machines. By portraying his own dehumanization in outrageous extremes, Lacombe creates a savage comedy of excess.

In Lacombe's most ingenious clown routine he plays the role of an orchestra conductor reduced to conducting the electronic reproduction of a symphony as heard through the speakers of an amplified Sony Walkman. He begins by trying to read a handwritten musical score, but the pages keep falling off the music stand, so he tosses away the score and places himself at the mercy of the Walkman. To enable the audience to hear the symphony, Lacombe places the headphones on a microphone, creating the ludicrous picture of music passing directly from one machine to another without the inconvenience of human intervention.

Lacombe's comic portrait of a man losing his soul to machines reaches new levels of absurdity as he shackles his boots into a specially constructed conductor's podium. The device enables Lacombe's body to shift with the waving of his baton. The music is Tchaikovsky's "1812 Overture," and every change in tempo is accompanied by a matching change in Lacombe's movements. As the music swirls through the loudspeakers, the clown's body gyrates under the whirling of his baton. The circles he makes are gravitationally impossible, but Lacombe is possessed by the pulses of the music, and the hidden springs in his mechanical podium give him a spectacularly acrobatic freedom. He rides the music as if he

were skiing down a mountain of sound, his body responding to all the hills and valleys of the musical terrain.

But at the same time that Lacombe is liberated by his mechanical podium, he is its prisoner. As the pace of the music builds, the clown is swept away by its intensity, losing control of his body in the whirlwind of Tchaikovsky's crescendos. He is not conducting the music. The music is conducting him. Or to be more precise, the electronic reproduction of the music is conducting him. Lacombe's bouncing body is at the mercy of the Walkman's idiosyncracies. When the battery power fades and the music slows down to a crawl, the clown's body drops into a listless shape of horizontal helplessness. Every recorded glitch dictates an erratic spasm of movement. When the recording begins repeating itself, so does Lacombe, throwing his baton in the air over and over again as if his body were a broken record.

Lacombe's hilarious physicalization of technology gone haywire acquires a special resonance when performed in the context of Cirque du Soleil's high-tech aesthetics. He performed the same routine with the Big Apple Circus during the 1986-87 season, but feels that their audiences never responded as strongly as do those of Cirque du Soleil, where Lacombe's performance stops the show and often receives a standing ovation. His lunatic battle with technology touches a collective nerve with audiences whose senses have been primed by synthesizer music and high-speed circus montage. At the slower-paced Big Apple Circus, Lacombe was just an eccentric funnyman. At Cirque du Soleil he is an electronic court jester, whose struggle with forces beyond his control seems more urgently related to his immediate surroundings.

It is not surprising that Lacombe's comedy is so well suited to Cirque du Soleil. He studied clowning at the Ecole Nationale du Cirque du Montreal, which is run by Guy Caron, artistic director of Cirque du Soleil. Lacombe began performing with Cirque du Soleil immediately after graduating from the Montreal circus school in 1985. He was twenty-eight years old and has been with Cirque du Soleil

DENIS LACOMBE.

at least part of every season since then. Lacombe's role models include silent film artists like Keaton and Chaplin. He also admires the slapstick antics of Jerry Lewis. When Lacombe won the bronze medal for clowning at the International Circus Festival in Monte Carlo in 1985, one of the participants told him that his routines seemed to satirize the overstated style of American physical comedy that Europeans remember from the Jerry Lewis movies of the fifties and sixties. Actually, Lacombe had no intention of satirizing Lewis. He simply shares Lewis's taste for physical excess. Lacombe's attraction to extremes coincides neatly with the needs of Cirque du Soleil. In the midst of all the high-tech action and sound, the only way for an individual to get himself noticed is to engage in acts of wild physicality.

As the orchestra conductor, Lacombe responds to the mechanized music and podium with a manic fury that demands the audience's attention. He uses the same extreme style in his portrayal of a robot clown activated by a mock remote-control transmitter. Once the clown gets into gear he begins searching for extreme forms of comic stimulation. Whenever he falls down or is disappointed, he consoles himself by spinning a wheel of feathers under his armpit. He responds to the mechanical tickling with shrieks of laughter, and then continues his activities. Like all good citizens of technological wonderlands the clown has learned to erase his pain with an artificial pleasure device that allows him to indulge in the uninterrupted pursuit of personal satisfaction.

Dressed in a pink clown wig and a hideous orange costume, Lacombe's robot clown is a nightmarish vision of overstimulation. Elbow pads give his outfit the feel of a hockey player's uniform. The pointed hat looks like some absurd piece of combat gear. All aspects of Lacombe's grotesque uniform suggest that he practices a profession that encourages self-destruction. He fulfills this expectation by assaulting himself with pies.

Like a refugee from a Mack Sennett comedy gone berserk, Lacombe hurls pies in his own face with relentless precision. The sequence starts out accidentally,

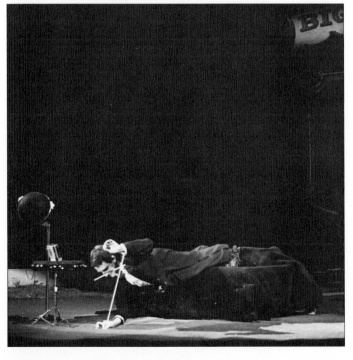

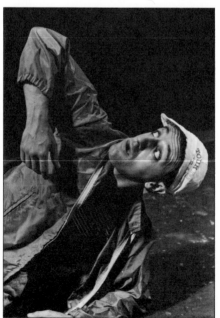

when a pie he is balancing on a tube falls off onto his face. Lacombe comforts himself with the mechanical tickler and pulls another pie out of his trunk. But instead of trying to balance this one, he throws it at himself, taking perverse pleasure in the self-inflicted injury. The more he tries it, the more he likes it. The robot clown becomes obsessed with finding new ways to hit himself with pies. He falls flat on his belly so that his face lands on a pie he has strategically placed on the ground underneath him. Howling with laughter, he jumps on the end of a diagonally balanced teeterboard, catapulting the pie on the other end directly into his face. The clown is addicted to the pies as if they were drugs. He finally straps a lever-like contraption onto his chest that throws pies automatically.

Lacombe aims the automatic pie-throwing machine at the audience, but the assistant operating the remote-control device adjusts the command, so that the robot clown aims the machine at himself instead. As in the clown conductor routine, Lacombe defies technology at the same time that he capitulates to it. The robot clown is a slapstick machine designed to create automatic laughter in a high-tech circus, but he refuses to settle into ordinary mechanical patterns. Lacombe asserts his independence by obeying the rules with a vengeance. If the circus demands that he perform demeaning slapstick to win the audience's attention, then he wills himself to take the simplest act of slapstick to excessive extremes. He defies the external tyranny of his mechanical masters by tyrannizing himself more violently than they could possibly imagine. The man with the remote control merely wanted the robot clown to redirect the pie from the audience towards himself. Lacombe went further. He hit himself with the same pie over and over again, marching out of the ring as he victoriously pelted himself with a mechanical viciousness that no machine could match. Finding wild joy in an orgy of self-stimulation, the robot clown is as ridiculous, unnerving, exasperating and un-fathomable as a Jerry Lewis telethon.

The other acts that Lacombe performs in Cirque du Soleil are equally savage in their pursuit of slapstick extremes. In one routine Lacombe is attacked by an

DENIS LACOMBE
FIGHTING THE
INVISIBLE MAN.

invisible man. For five minutes the audience watches the bizarre spectacle of a man who seems to be slapping himself through space, spinning himself in circles, and hurling himself into the ground. The violence of the self-inflicted barrage of pies seems mild in comparison to the physical brutality of Lacombe's encounter with his invisible combatant. Treading the border between black humor and grotesque tragedy, Lacombe keeps the piece funny by recovering from each new onslaught without evidence of pain. Like the eternally straight-faced Buster Keaton, Lacombe responds to his bone-crushing falls with deadpan nonchalance. Again, Cirque du Soleil's high-powered environment gives added poignance to the comedy. The clown has no more hope of defeating the faceless nemesis ambushing him from all sides than the acrobats have of slowing down the circus's relentless tempo, but Lacombe fascinates us with the quiet dignity he displays in his battle against impossible odds.

Denis Lacombe is an old-fashioned clown lost in a new-wave circus. With physical comedy as his only weapon, he wages a slapstick war against the electronic powers that seem intent on stealing his autonomy. In mortal comic combat with Sony Walkmen, remote-controlled pies and invisible wrestlers, Lacombe demonstrates the tenacity of the human spirit through his indefatigable ability to withstand punishment. Battered by the music, slapped senseless by the pies, and brutalized by the invisible gladiator, Lacombe keeps the audience laughing simply by managing to survive. While everything else in Cirque du Soleil is slickly orchestrated and electronically satisfying, Lacombe's clowning provides short-circuited unpredictability. The rhythms pulsing through the maestro's muscles and the electrons coursing through the robot's body suggest that the clown has been consumed by technology, but Lacombe maintains his human identity through the fierceness of his physical exertion. The wild intensity of his physical action signals that he is battling for his soul.

By the end of the show, the audience at Cirque du Soleil has been whipped up to a rock-concert frenzy by the fast-paced montage of performances, lights and synthesizers. When it is time for the troupe of comic bunglers that opened the show to give up their flashy costumes and return to the mundane world they inhabited before the circus began, the spectators in the tent register their disappointment. "I don't want it to be over," moans a woman behind me, expressing the collective sentiments of the crowd. They have all been charged up by the electronic stimulation of the event, and are made to feel dismayed at the prospect of being thrust back into the low-tech environment of their ordinary lives.

Nevertheless, the bunglers return to their rags, and the glittery performers disappear into a manufactured haze of dry ice and soft light. The good-bye is staged in a way that elicits feelings of regret, so that the curtain call becomes a joyous emotional reprieve. The synthesizer music surges in volume, the lights flash brightly in the mist, and the performers rush back into the ring with an exuberant burst of energy. A standing ovation is almost obligatory.

The manipulative curtain call is a fitting conclusion to a show where performers and audience alike are asked to surrender themselves to the seductive rhythms of a music-video wonderland. As the spectacle ends, our sense of loss recalls the sadness in Dorothy's farewell to her friends in Oz, when she leaves the world of technicolor for the drabness of black-and-white Kansas. But the ending of Cirque du Soleil is a 1980s reversal of the central theme in *The Wizard of Oz*. Instead of feeling that there is no place like home, we are left believing that there is no place like Oz—or in this case, the circus. After the thrills of a technicolor fantasyland, the world beyond the circus tent seems like a letdown. We have become addicted to special effects, and the multimedia curtain call is designed to give us one last fix.

For the finale a simulated sun is projected onto the curtain at the entrance to the ring. Cirque du Soleil means circus of the sun, and this final image is a teasing reminder of the electronic pleasures that will always remain somewhere over the rainbow. As the performers wave good-bye, Denis Lacombe stands apart from the sentimental conclusion. Unlike the others, he seems relieved at the unplugging of this supercharged spectacle. All through the show

Lacombe has defied his music-video environment and he maintains his stance of revolt to the end. His response to a society of high-tech junkies has been to develop a style of physical comedy that takes the conflict between technology and the body to its most outrageous extremes. Lacombe's slapstick convulsions are both comic and desperate, a clown's reaction to a severe case of electronic overdose.

Avner The Eccentric

"By admonishing latecomers at the beginning of the show and taking
their picture I'm planting a hypnotic suggestion which says, you
may be watching a play, but we're watching you, and you are part
of the dialogue now. If you do something, it's going to be part of
the performance. You thought you could just come and sit and be
the Broadway audience. No. You're the audience, and you've
got work to do."

—AVNER THE ECCENTRIC

While projecting the image of a maladroit bungler, Avner the Eccentric manipulates both props and audiences with the deft precision of a slapstick engineer. Every drop of a hat, every gasp of the crowd, every hum of his kazoo is calculated to give the illusion of spontaneity, when in fact it has been carefully planned by a clown who is a master of physical and psychological control. Avner wears the black beard and ragged clothes of a traditional tramp clown, but he has reinvented the archetypal figure into a character who embodies our era's prevailing forms of duplicity. His comic technique mirrors the disingenuous managerial style of high-level administrators and politicians who project a nonchalant amiability that masks a shrewd understanding of power and its consequences.

The silent prologue to the Lincoln Center production of *The Comedy of Errors* captures the central paradox of Avner's comedy in fundamental terms of failure and success. The clown walks onto the empty stage pushing a broom, as if he were a lowly janitor getting things ready for the Shakespearean actors to follow. When he stops sweeping to take a smoking break, the cigarettes drop all over the stage. As he bends over to pick them up, his matches spill out of their box and his broom falls apart. The failures of the hapless stagehand are orchestrated in rising crescendos of ineptitude, so that the props seem to be engaged in an organized revolt. His comic struggle climaxes with an attempt to retrieve his hat from the top of the broomstick. He tries to balance the stick on his forehead, but it falls. This seeming defeat turns into victory when the hat pops off the stick and lands miraculously on his head. Following the pathetic mishandling of everything he touches, the clown's sudden act of dexterity is so astonishing that the crowd breaks into delighted applause.

Before the applause, Avner pretends not to notice the audience, but his stage innocence is part of the act and once he receives their affirmation the clown launches into a phase of his performance that is even more astonishing than his masterful manipulation of objects: his masterful manipulation of the public.

Avner is as deliberate in shaping the responses of his audience as he is in shaping the trajectory of his falling props. The clown appears to be at the mercy of random events; he is in fact skillfully calculating their outcome.

The key to Avner's successful management of both people and props is his shrewd understanding of equilibrium. When he balances a broom on his nose, the need for equilibrium is obvious. The concept is subtler when he plays with the public. The clown uses a variety of comic techniques to mildly disrupt the equilibrium of the relationship between the audience and the stage. Once the audience is off balance, they are far more malleable to his unspoken suggestions than they would be if the typical actor-audience rapport had been left undisturbed. At Lincoln Center, for example, he interrupted the applause for his hat trick to admonish latecomers. Up until this time, the audience had been permitted to retain their anonymity, but Avner's comic business with those who arrive late is a signal that their actions are being watched from the stage. He emphasizes the point by removing an Instamatic from his pocket and photographing the tardy spectators as they take their seats. The tactic redefines his relationship with the crowd. While the audience laughs at his surveillance, they begin to shift their senses from a state of one-way observation to two-way alert.

Subverting the public's expectations about attending Shakespeare at Lincoln Center, Avner continued to keep them off balance by taking more photographs, leaping off the stage and sitting on a spectator's lap. Then he deepened the level of involvement by giving people his camera and suggesting that they photograph him. He never speaks, but his wishes are clear, and the audience eagerly complies. Like a good manager, Avner has set up a situation in which at least a partial sense of equilibrium can be restored if the audience member takes the action the clown demands. The implicit contract is that if the spectator is obedient and takes the snapshot, Avner will get back up on the stage where he belongs.

Eventually he does return to the stage, where he sweeps the debris from his act down a trap door, out of which emerges the figure of Shakespeare carrying the text of the play covered with the dirt from Avner's broom. The slapstick trashing of Shakespeare has begun, and the audience has become an accomplice to the crime. They have committed themselves to active participation in Avner's shenanigans, and with the battle lines drawn between high art and low, the public has been won over to the side of the clown. Director Robert Woodruff noted that preview audiences did not warm up to the play as quickly as they did once Avner's prologue was included. The clown's warmup is so successful that the audience responds vocally to the first-act performers who ask if Antipholus and Dromio of Syracuse deserve a pie in the face as punishment for badly delivered puns. The public's verdict was a resounding yes, and the pies were dutifully delivered to the poor punsters. This rare instance of interactive Shakespeare can be directly attributed to the bond between audience and stage action that Avner established in the opening moments of the show.

Avner elicits audience participation to an even greater extent in the one-man show he has presented on Broadway and around the world. Here again the clown creates the illusion of failure by letting his props seem to get the best of him, but he also displays surprising dexterity by juggling baseball bats, walking the slack rope and balancing a ladder on his chin. His entertaining triumphs over inanimate objects are interspersed with a series of equally impressive triumphs over audience volunteers. As usual his manipulative skills are subtle, gentle and extraordinarily effective. Avner gets the volunteers to come onstage and participate in his act by creating situations in which the most comfortable choices they can make are precisely the choices he wants them to make. As he does in his physical balancing acts, Avner creates the comic illusion that he is losing control, when in fact everything is occurring precisely according to plan.

The relationship between Avner and his audience is mirrored in the relationship between Avner and his props. A good example is his extended duet with a red cloth napkin. The clown rolls the napkin into a tube-like shape with a knot at the end that makes it look like some kind of elongated puppy. Avner tries to caress the hot-dog creature in his arms, but it keeps hopping out of his grasp. The napkin appears to be alive, and taking actions that confound the desires of the clown, when it is actually his hidden finger movements that animate the cloth. Further manipulations of the napkin give it the appearance of having a substantial form, and Avner actually manages to use it for support while doing a handstand. A moment later the napkin collapses, and the clown falls. The object seems to be defying him, but every detail is carefully choreographed, from the well-timed collapse of the handstand to the wiping of his brow.

The same style of invisibly structured anarchy prevails in Avner's comic inter-actions with his audience volunteers. The onstage arrival of someone from the audience creates the expectation that anything can happen. Nothing is rehearsed. Avner has never met the volunteer before. The theatre is filled with a charged atmosphere of anticipation. How will the performer cope with the unplanned responses of his new collaborator? As it turns out, Avner handles the situation masterfully. In spite of the fact that the volunteer does not know what to expect, and Avner never says a word, the interaction inevitably follows the same pattern in every show. Maintaining an air of improvisation, Avner subtly guides the performance in a direction that will result in a cascade of surefire laughter.

Avner is always careful to make the experience pleasant for his impromptu partners. The first volunteer, usually a woman, is given a present, an origami unicorn that Avner sculpts out of paper on the spot. Having won her trust, Avner nonverbally directs her to hold her two index fingers out in front of her chest. She complies, and Avner inserts a roll of toilet paper between her outstretched digits. She joins in the audience laughter at the unexpected turn of events, but Avner insures her continued participation with supportive gestures and sounds. Every time she carries out one of Avner's simple requests, he makes her feel like a success. The audience applauds her regularly, and she is eager to keep the approval coming.

Eventually Avner starts unrolling the toilet paper from her fingers and rolling it into little wads. He shows each wad to her and then makes her believe it has disappeared. Actually Avner throws it over her head and behind her, but the action is done so quickly and close to her face that only the audience can see what is really happening. With every new disappearance, the volunteer registers the shock of disbelief, and the audience laughs at the clown's blatant act of comic deception. The volunteer is clearly the victim of the joke, but she laughs along with the audience, assuming that they are as amazed by Avner's magical powers as she is. Avner heightens the deliberate confusion by asking questions through a kazoo. With the indistinct humming sounds of the kazoo he seems to be asking the volunteer, "Where did it go?" When she responds with gestures of bewilderment, Avner turns to the audience with a burst of kazoo noise that says, "She didn't see it."

Each time the disappearing action is repeated, it is accompanied by the two-line kazoo refrain. The situation gets funnier and funnier, because Avner is shouting out loud that he is fooling her, but she doesn't understand the meaning of his exclamations. The pace quickens, and the wads of toilet paper get bigger and bigger, making it more and more astonishing that the volunteer can't see them fly over her head. In mock desperation, Avner removes his trousers, rolls them into a ball and throws them over her head with an action too obvious to be missed. She looks behind her, sees the wads of paper, and is finally let in on the joke that the audience has been laughing at all along. There is a communal laughter of recognition; Avner hugs her; the audience applauds her; and she returns to her seat with the origami unicorn.

Avner's handling of the situation is impressive. His managerial skills are worthy of a top-level corporate executive. The volunteer is used as a human toilet-paper dispenser; the audience laughs at her ignorance; Avner guides her into doing exactly what he wants her to do; but she leaves the stage feeling good about her participation in the event, without a trace of humiliation. Considering the complexity of the psychology involved, it is not surprising to learn that one of Avner's

major influences was a hypnotherapist. Avner says that hypnotherapists occasionally come up to him after the show to comment on the similarity between his art and their profession.

The traditional slapstick aspects of Avner's show derive from the clown characterization techniques he learned as a student of Jacques Lecoq in the early 1970s. Lecoq's technique stresses physical skills and object manipulation in the creation of comic characters. Avner has learned these lessons well, but what sets his performance apart from the hundreds of other Lecoq graduates who perform physical comedy is his shrewd ability to manipulate the audience as effortlessly as he manipulates his body and his props. Many clowns can do a back flip. Many more can balance feathers on their noses. But few can direct the outcome of audience response with Avner's delicate touch.

Like the hypnotherapists whose work he has studied, Avner works with suggestions rather than commands. The woman with the toilet paper between her fingers is never ordered to look straight ahead of her, but Avner sets up the situation so that a series of almost imperceptible suggestions makes it highly unlikely that she would turn around and discover the paper wads. All his movements and kazoo sounds direct her attention forward. Only when he throws his pants behind her does he stop his downstage distractions and give her nonverbal permission to turn around. She follows his unspoken suggestion, looks upstage, and gives him the response of recognition he is looking for to get a final laugh from the audience and bring the routine to a close.

The spirit of the interaction is playful. There is nothing cruel or derisive about the audience's laughter; they are laughing at the spectacle of deception, taking pleasure in the game Avner is playing with the volunteer. They are also expressing their admiration for Avner's dexterity in avoiding detection. Earlier in the show Avner won the audience's sympathy in his struggles with inanimate cups, bats and stepladders, living out the fantasies of everyone in the theatre who had ever come out on the losing end of a battle with a leaky faucet or a precariously balanced stack of dishes. The audience cheered as he triumphantly juggled and balanced the mundane objects that had originally posed him such difficulties. Their response to the way Avner manipulates his volunteers is similarly enthusiastic. Everyone wishes they could persuade people to do without resentment what they ask them to do. Avner provides a comic model of mind control, but because it lasts for only a few harmless minutes on the stage, it can be called by the less sinister name of clown control.

The element of manipulation in Avner's act becomes more explicit when he brings children onstage as volunteers in the second part of the show. He literally moves them around like puppets. One child's arm is raised up and down to make it look like he is interminably trying to shake Avner's hand. Another has his torso bobbed up and down as Avner molds his body into a continuous bow that draws ever-increasing amounts of laughter and applause. Avner spins still another child around in circles, throwing him off balance so that he leans back against Avner's legs when he comes to rest. Here again, Avner plays ingeniously with his understanding of equilibrium. Avner supports the child's tottering weight with his legs just long enough to make him comfortable. Then he steps away, causing the child to fall backwards. Avner catches him before he falls, but then steps back again, throwing the child off balance once more. The effect is comical, giving the illusion that Avner is continually rescuing a child who has lost the ability to stand on his own two feet. The actual situation, of course, is quite different. Avner is in complete control of the child's every movement. The clown hugs and kisses the child to the applause of the audience before sending him back to his seat, and there are no hard feelings involved, but the interaction epitomizes what Avner does so expertly throughout his performance. He alternately wins and betrays the trust of his volunteers, masking the paradox of his strategy in the affirming laughter of the spectators, who see the encounter as a spontaneous improvised event.

By the end of the performance, Avner has moved his comedy into a realm markedly different from the place it began. First, he has broken down the barrier between actor and public, giving the audience the role of active participants who are fully invested in urging him on to success. But even more importantly, his character has graduated from the status of a helpless tramp to that of a master of physical and social control. Initially he had to struggle to keep from being overwhelmed by paper cups, dinner napkins and baseball bats that seemed determined to do him in. By the time the show closes he has overcome all the obstacles he has encountered. The possibility of his failing diminishes significantly with each new routine he presents, until the final bits are more like pure exhibition of skills than battles with the specter of defeat. At the beginning of the show the audience worries about Avner's ability to survive, but they leave the theatre with their pity transformed to awe.

The impressive routines with which Avner closes the show are about eating and drinking. Traditionally down-and-out clowns have focused on themes of hunger and thirst. At the opening of the show, one might have imagined Avner's tramp character performing the classic commedia dell'arte sketch about a servant who eats a fly to stave off starvation. But by the end of the evening Avner's successes have made him resemble a master much more than a servant. And in fact Avner's concluding food routines are displays of overindulgence. His character is so far removed from the possibility of thirst that he makes a show of how much water he can spit out of his mouth. Then the clown moves on to a hilarious ingestion of dozens of napkins, again without the suggestion of real need, but simply to demonstrate how many napkins he is capable of making us believe he has swallowed. In a striking inversion of the comic theme of hunger, Avner's tramp turned aristocrat demurely polishes off a few dozen white napkins and spits them out in the form of paper streamers that have absorbed the color of his wine. He tops it all off by belching up a bouquet of paper flowers. The sequence suggests a guest at a bizarrely posh dinner party. Having begun his performance with the travails of a common tramp, Avner ends it with a yuppie's burp. His virtuosic skills of manipulation have metamorphosed his character into an upwardly mobile clown whose powers of control extend from the intricacies of social management to the polite mastery of his bodily functions. Avner has clearly remolded the tramp clown into a figure that is appropriate to America in the eighties, and his final moment on stage confirms the aptness of his vision. He replaces hunger with gluttony in a sketch about a man who eats things he doesn't want or need, while the audience displays their approval of his conspicuous consumption with a burst of applause for his regurgitated paper bouquet.

PICKLE FAMILY CIRCUS

"The idea of family extends even beyond the large group of Pickles past

and present. It reaches out and embraces the audience, and the

sponsors, and the towns that we visit. Cousin Pickle is in town. We're

like the crazy uncle that comes to visit once a year, and tells jokes and

sings songs and does tricks. And you're always sorry when he's gone."

—PEGGY SNIDER

If you crossbred a Norman Rockwell family with a Karl Marx collective, and gave everyone lessons in acrobatics, the resulting clan might look a lot like the Pickle Family Circus. The Pickles are a one-ring embodiment of an ideal community struggling to make a place for itself in an imperfect world. The jugglers, tumblers, gymnasts and clowns are engagingly wholesome in their efforts to create an ensemble circus performance. Rejecting the star system, the artists are so democratically supportive of one another that they serve as each other's stagehands when not engaged in acts of their own. At a typical Pickle Family show one might see a trampoline performer hold the rosin bag for a trapezist, or a tightrope walker carry on the juggler's props.

The egalitarian feel of the Pickle Circus encourages the audience to believe that any group of people can achieve a common goal with enough hard work and cooperation. The performers have the clean-cut look of an ordinary extended family whose members just happen to have the ability to stand on each other's shoulders, balance chairs on their chins, and turn somersaults in mid-air. The young woman who swings from the high trapeze is an airborne image of the beautifully poised and resourceful daughter that everyone would love to have in their family. The youthful duo bouncing on the trampoline could be brother and sister, demonstrating an admirable sensitivity to each other's needs as they execute difficult stunts requiring split-second timing. A gymnastic balancing act is performed by a mother-daughter team who seem to be transforming their problem-free relationship into a smooth, muscular dance number.

The paterfamilias of this unusual collective is a clown, Larry Pisoni, who performs many of his skits with his ten-year old son Lorenzo. One of the founders of the circus, and the show's most frequently reappearing character, Pisoni is clearly the leader of the clan. As the father figure of the democratically minded Pickles he takes on the delicate task of trying to guide the members of his young troupe without imposing his will on them. Behind the scenes he is their director. Onstage he plays the role of a slightly befuddled autocrat who is continually

MARC JONDALL.

thwarted in his gentle efforts to create a sense of order in the ring. His wishes are met with mild defiance from free spirits waving banners and wearing gorilla suits, but in the end a sense of harmony always prevails. The resilience of the family is further demonstrated by their ability to perform without Pisoni when he takes sabbaticals to pursue other projects.

Pisoni founded the Pickle Family Circus with Peggy Snider, the company's manager, technical director and costume designer, in 1974. They met while working together in the San Francisco Mime Troupe. Snider had already been with the Mime Troupe for three years when Pisoni arrived in 1971 from New York, where he studied circus skills with Hovey Burgess and Judy Finelli at a club called the Electric Circus. Pisoni was responsible for introducing juggling into the arsenal of political-satire techniques used by the Mime Troupe. Although the company was receptive to the use of such skills in their repertoire, it would clearly never become a full-fledged circus, so Pisoni and Snider left to form one. They brought with them the social ideals of the Mime Troupe, but chose to leave behind the overt rhetoric of political theatre. The Pickle Family's message is implicit in the nonverbal structure of its presentation. There are no animal acts, and no suggestion of the ownership, humiliation and domination with which they are often associated. Women do not assume submissive roles in the routines and their bodies are not exploited as objects of display. The circus manifests its values in its demonstrations of skill, cooperation and interdependence.

The principles of the circus are also expressed by the creative ways in which it is financed. Each stop of a typical Pickle Family tour is sponsored by a local community group, often using the event to raise money for such things as day-care centers or homes for senior citizens. Consequently those who attend these performances have bought their tickets in support of a particular cause and are working together towards a common end simply by attending the circus. This situation creates an unspoken bond between audience and performers, emphasizing their common concern.

The links between the audience and the circus are reinforced by the informality of the seating arrangements. The Pickles usually perform outdoors under the open sky, with the adult audience seated in portable grandstands and the children encouraged to sit on the grass up close to the performers. Pisoni opens the show with a clown routine that immediately involves the children in his comic efforts to hold onto helium balloons. Like the circus family he can never keep entirely under his control, the balloons keep escaping from his grip to follow colorful paths of their own into the sky. As they drift away Pisoni is chased offstage by the entire cast of the Pickle Family Circus—leaping, waving banners, turning cartwheels, dancing acrobatically to the spirited live music of the Pickle Family Jazz Band. When Pisoni reenters the scene, it is to engage the audience in a game of catch with a balloon bigger than he is. The clown's efforts end with the floating sphere exploding on his head, but despite this setback Pisoni leaves the ring having established himself as the bumbling master of ceremonies for the afternoon's attempts to bring people together.

Shortly Pisoni returns to do an acrobatic clown dance with his son, Lorenzo. Performed entirely without words, their scenario plays like a slapstick version of *Father Knows Best*. Pisoni tries to teach Lorenzo how to do a back flip, urging him to generate momentum by taking a running leap into his father's hands. After a few comic failures, Pisoni's patient teaching results in success, and Lorenzo gleefully bows to the audience applause, leaving his father in the shadows.

This filial hubris leads to a pantomime lecture from the father clown about the importance of acknowledging both halves of the team. Lorenzo hangs his head in shame but soon forgets the lesson, and incites the band to disobey his father by playing a jazz tune that Pisoni dislikes. Lorenzo dances a neat little soft-shoe to the melody in spite of his father's reproaches, and eventually the two of them are boogeying together in a goofy rubber-limbed duet that epitomizes the resolution of their differences. Their new-found harmony is signified by a pair of back flips executed in perfect synchrony. Jauntily waving goodbye to the crowd, father and

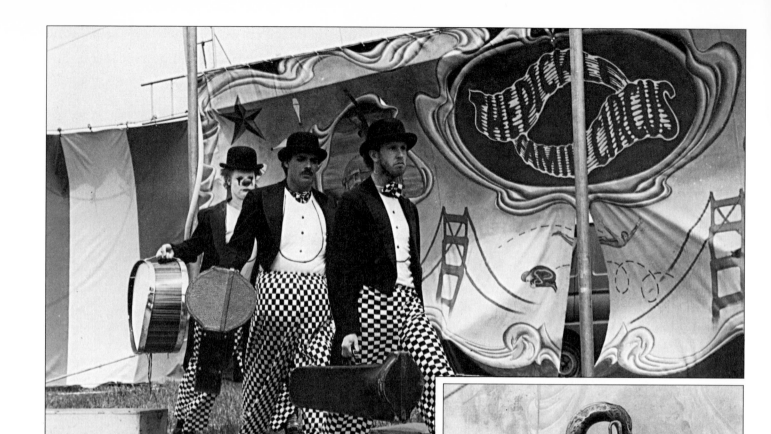

BILL IRWIN, LARRY PISONI AND GEOFF HOYLE.

GEOFF HOYLE.

son share the audience's acclamation in equal measure, each having learned the value of the other's contributions to the act.

Another Pickle Family clown routine explores a more mythic dimension of the father-son relationship by recreating the classic story of Giupetto the puppet maker and his wooden creation that comes to life. Pisoni opens the piece with a child-sized dummy as his slapstick partner, but poignantly conveys his longing for a flesh-and-blood son with whom he could truly share the tricks of his trade. When his dream comes true and Lorenzo emerges from a trunk as a real child with a will of his own, Pisoni teaches his son classic clown gags that range from interrupted handshakes to acrobatic pratfalls. A true chip off the old block, Lorenzo learns the bits so well that he often fools his father with well-timed moves of physical misdirection. Pisoni's fatherly elation at his prodigy's mastery of the craft is made all the more touching by the knowledge that the clown duo is a genuine father-and-son team.

Not all the clown routines in the Pickle Family Circus reflect family relations in such neatly ordered terms. One of the classic Pickle capers involves a bevy of dancing gorillas. Originally choreographed by Kimi Okada in 1983, the surrealistic encounter between Pisoni and the terpsichorean apes has been revived numerous times in subsequent years. The action begins innocently enough, with a baby gorilla sneaking out of a trunk behind Pisoni's back and doing a tap dance while the clown is out of sight. Hearing the taps, Pisoni returns, only to be assaulted by increasing numbers of progressively larger gorillas, all wearing identical ruffed collars with red polka dots. In a dazzling display of simian acrobatics they jump on top of him, leap over him, bound into his arms, and hop in and out of trunks. Unable to combat or contain the apes, Pisoni ends up joining them in a hairy-legged version of a Rockette chorus line.

There is no clear story line or logic to the absurd antics of the dancing gorillas, but it is clear from their varied heights—pint-sized to oversized—and their matching collars that they constitute some kind of strange family unit. (The

LARRY AND
LORENZO PISONI.

wearers of the gorilla costumes in this piece have included Pisoni's son, step-daughter Gypsy, and former juggling teacher Judy Finelli.) Performing a pot-pourri of difficult stunts and intricate choreography, the eccentric clan of gorillas confirms the Pickle philosophy that cooperation can help a family accomplish anything its collective heart desires. Undaunted by the fact that they are only apes, the gorillas overcome opposition from Pisoni, and manage to live out their dancing fantasies on stage. They continue to delight the audience with astonishing demonstrations of unexpected panache, right up to the final curtain call when they climb into a gorilla variation of a "human pyramid," the ultimate expression of simian solidarity.

The Pickles present themselves as a family, complete with all the rites of passage inherent in family life. There are marriages and separations among the Pickle Family veterans. Babies have been born while the company is on the road. (One year three Pickle mothers were pregnant at the same time.) Members of the family move away, and return for visits. Ordinary families capture moments of transition in photographs. The Pickles mark them with public circus spectacles.

When Bill Irwin and Geoff Hoyle, two of the Pickle Family's most popular alumni, came back to carouse with their former colleagues in 1986, the event was memorialized by a reunion performance in an indoor proscenium theatre. Pisoni, Hoyle and Irwin recreated some of their old routines and invented new ones just for the occasion, stealing the spotlight from one another one minute and falling into the orchestra pit the next. Like playfully jealous siblings they alternately duped and rescued each other in a collaborative effort that ultimately had them dancing together in syncopated slapstick harmony. The San Francisco audience cheered the trio as if the veterans of a fabled championship team had been reunited for one last game.

In the late seventies, when Irwin, Hoyle and Pisoni were performing together regularly in the Pickle Family Clown Alley, they supported each other with admirable generosity, playing off each other's strengths to create moments of

LARRY PISONI
(LORENZO PICKLE) AND
GEOFF HOYLE
(MR. SNIFF).

physical ensemble comedy rooted in the nurturing environment of the Pickle Family fold. As an oddball white-faced clown named Willy, Irwin choreographed eccentric dances that seemed lighter than air. Hoyle's sausage-nosed and fiery-tempered Mr. Sniff initiated ridiculous confrontations with his partners and the audience. Baffled by this pair of wacky subordinates, Pisoni's robust clown-leader character found himself constantly and comically under seige. Whether the trio were playing musicians in a clown band or workers in an Italian restaurant, the conflicts in their group routines had the feel of friendly squabbles in a wacky family business.

Most veterans of the Pickle Family Circus, from clowns and aerialists to technicians and box office managers, have participated at one time or another in the legendary ritual of collective effort known as the Big Juggle. This spectacular exhibition of solid teamwork is the piece de resistance of every Pickle performance. Somewhere around a dozen Pickles grab three clubs each and pass them to one another in a dazzling variety of group formations. They pass over their backs in a continuously shifting line, and straight ahead towards the center of a semicircle. To increase the level of difficulty and the need for cooperation, all of them are balanced on rolling spheres.

Pisoni is usually the point man in this multileveled exhibition of juggling equilibristics. His senior position as a founder of the clan is acknowledged by his position at the center of the semicircle, throwing and receiving clubs from each member of his family in turn, as his feet nimbly maneuver the sphere in a manner that slowly rotates his body, lining him up with each new partner. Pisoni's adopted children dutifully feed him passes that move the routine along, but when he turns to Lorenzo at the end of the sequence, his son puts on a display of comic obstinence that delays the conclusion of the show. When Lorenzo gives in to his father's will and the urging of his circus siblings, the show closes with a juggling metaphor for filial obedience and cooperative family spirit.

Although Pisoni is at the physical center of the Big Juggle, the exhibition is offered as a demonstration of the ensemble's ability to work towards a common goal. In each element of the routine's many interlocking segments members of the family are focusing on keeping the chain of juggling clubs moving. One juggler throws a little higher and slower to compensate for an overturned spin thrown by someone else. Another juggler throwing to a partner shorter than herself is careful to toss the clubs especially low to avoid an injury that could be caused by catching a club too close to the head. Countless details of speed, trajectory and positioning are rushing through everyone's mind as dozens of clubs fly through the air, but the focus of everyone's concentration is the same: doing your part to keep the effort going and make the group look good.

Whether they are backstage setting up each other's equipment or spotting each other's aerial acrobatics as part of a human safety net, the Pickles project the image of a tight-knit clan whose members care about each other. Their circus appeals strongly to the contemporary public's desire to reconcile old-world ideals of family togetherness with new-age visions of free-spirited family democracy.

In their mythic presentation of a family of acrobats, jugglers and clowns who dance, laugh and fly through the air together, the Pickles seem to have it all. Performing intimate acts of acrobatics with their offspring, the mothers have their careers, their beauty, and their children too. The fathers guide their sons, and teach them skills, but know when to give them the freedom to improvise on their own. The whole family pulls together in common efforts, but not in a way that suffocates the endeavors of each individual. The idiosyncratic contributions of all family members, whether they choose to dance in gorilla costumes or hang from a swinging trapeze by their toes, are lovingly embraced, and proudly introduced to the public as a continuation of family tradition.

By the time the show is over, everybody in the audience wishes they had a father

MR. SNIFF AND WILLY
THE CLOWN.

who could do pratfalls, a mother who could juggle, a sister who could do back flips in the air, a brother who could walk on his hands. The circus skills displayed by the troupe are admirable, but it is the simple, decent family values inherent in their execution that make the show unique. Other circuses make you dream of running away to join them. The family spirit of the Pickles makes you dream of bringing the circus home with you when you leave.

SPALDING GRAY

"I like to think of myself as a kind of 'poetic reporter,' more like an impressionist painter than a photographer. Most reporters get the facts out as quickly as possible—fresh news is the best news. I do just the opposite. I give the facts a chance to settle down until at last they blend, bubble and mix in the swamp of dream, memory and reflection."

—SPALDING GRAY

Spalding Gray is a virtuoso rememberer. He takes raw memory and sculpts it into finely wrought performances of epic autobiography. Sitting at a table and talking directly to the audience, Gray performs feats of poetic recall that are remarkable in their clarity, resonance and wit. In a culture where collective memory has atrophied and been replaced by a television tube, audiences respond with rapt attention to the simple authenticity of Gray's personal chronicles.

There are moments in Gray's low-keyed monologues when he seems to be caught in the act of remembering. His voice and gestures create the impression that he is conjuring up the past as he speaks, as if his memory were leaving tangible traces of its efforts. The rhythm of his delivery is peppered with hesitations. The lines in his face wrinkle with concentration. His hands move out in front of him as if they are reaching for images on the verge of being forgotten. Although it all appears spontaneous and casual, each nuance is artfully crafted. Gray has mastered the art of self-performance so completely that even his stammers are planned.

In the process of giving his memories a physical shape, Gray sifts them through the filters of contemporary culture. His stories reach the audience through a series of prisms. Gray performs himself remembering himself, as if he were seeing himself in a movie or reading about himself in a newspaper or watching himself on television. His exercises in hyperautobiography are shaped by the popular media that dominate American society. Gray's stories reflect collective as well as personal anxieties. He remembers his past in terms of his relationships with other people and those relationships are mediated by the demands of their shared culture. Gray's stories are full of vivid portraits of people he has met, and each of those portraits is conveyed in a narrative style rooted in the rhetoric of mass communications. Gray is a one-man newspaper reporter, cinematic auteur and television talk-show host. His multiple roles give even his most intimate memories a sense of ironic detachment. He narrates his past like a man who has difficulty believing it, but is determined to re-play it in an effort to make sense of his era.

Gray began performing his autobiographical monologues as an outgrowth of his work with the Wooster Group at New York's Performing Garage. In 1975 the company began work on a trilogy of plays based on Gray's recollections of growing up in Rhode Island. The success of these ensemble productions led Gray to investigate the possibilities of performing his past as a sit-down monologist. The first of these efforts, *Sex and Death to the Age 14,* was presented at the Performing Garage in 1979. Since then he has performed the collected chronicles of his life in theatres all over the country. *A Personal History of the American Theatre* was broadcast on the PBS *Alive from Off Center* series. *Terrors of Pleasure* appeared on HBO. And *Swimming to Cambodia* was released in movie theatres as a feature film directed by Jonathan Demme.

The stories in Gray's monologues are always centered around his personal experiences, but he places them in the context of characters and events that mirror the rich landscape of American dreams and nightmares. *A Personal History of the American Theatre* is as much about the success ethic of American artists as it is about Gray's own life as an actor. Gray simply recounts stories about the plays in which he has performed, but he has worked in enough different settings to make his oral memoirs representative of the profession. He moves deftly from the excesses of Stanislavsky-styled realism in Texas regional theatre to avant-garde experiments with grunting and groping disciples of Grotowski in Manhattan, providing oblique insights into the state of the arts in America at the same time that he casts light on the origins of his own storytelling impulses. He says that as a child he discovered that acting things out was "a kind of ontological state. . . . Life was kind of boring for me in Barrington, Rhode Island, and I would dramatize it by taking any cue from life and blowing it up a bit, theatricalizing it." Theatricalization of his experiences includes putting them in a social and historical perspective. His childhood memories as retold in *Sex and Death to the Age 14* are framed by the atomic explosion at Hiroshima and the first test of the hydrogen bomb.

Swimming to Cambodia (1984) is an example of Gray's multileveled narrative style at its most complex. It began as a monologue about his involvement in *The Killing Fields*, a movie based on a magazine article about a war that most people saw only on television. Gray's performance technique is as densely textured as the layers of media memory in which the story has been wrapped. With a few maps and a pointer as his only props, Gray never moves from his chair, but he presents his tale in a style that subtly incorporates elements of each media through which the incidents have been recalled.

Gray opens the theatre version of his piece with a journalistic dateline: "Saturday, June 18, 1983. Gulf of Siam. Thailand." Then he fleshes out the details with verbal and gestural imagery that is cinematically arresting in its specificity. The colored maps he uses enable Gray to convey history and background information with the entertaining ease of a Sunday newspaper magazine supplement. And all the way through he cuts from one story fragment to another with the startling velocity of a television newsreel montage. Having assimilated the rhetorical devices of mass culture without losing the intimacy of old-fashioned storytelling, Spalding Gray transforms personal memory into a miniature spectacle with epic overtones.

While many performers have been reduced by entertainment technology into shells of vapid personality, Gray uses his understanding of mass media to sharpen his senses of perception and heighten his performance of the things he perceives. His gestures and vocal intonations are deeply influenced by the media through which his memories are filtered. Recounting the filming of a helicopter scene in *The Killing Fields*, Gray visually creates the sense of leaving the ground by tilting his head and torso. The illusion of television immediacy is furthered when he begins to shout as if his voice had to carry over the sound of the spinning copter blades. Shifting perspectives quickly, he paints word pictures of the jungle stretching out below him that are the equivalent of a cinematic long shot.

Gray's seemingly random jump cuts are carefully spliced into his monologues to provide the story with texture and resonance that transcend the cross-media grab-bag effect of the story's surface. A poetic writer with a vibrant sense of language, Gray creates cross references that are novelistic as well as cinematic. The tragicomic portrait of Thai peasants hired to imitate the Cambodian dead by smearing chicken blood on their bodies echoes an episode Gray spoke about a few minutes earlier. To pacify Cambodian villagers who had been accidentally bombed by American B-52s, U.S. Embassy officials gave out hundred-dollar bills to families of the dead and fifties to people who had lost arms or legs. Gray's deadpan juxtaposition of these two events satirizes the absurdity of equating the loss of limbs with a cash bonus. Linking the callous values of the filmmakers with those of the American government, Gray's disarmingly simple storytelling begins to assume the dimension of a spoken epic novel.

Gray's oral epic is full of sophisticated literary devices, but his performance language is informed with implicit references to modern media. The filmic quality of *Swimming to Cambodia* was established before Gray ever considered making a movie of the piece. Crosscutting, montage and closeups are embedded in the structure of Gray's visual memory and have nothing to do with Demme's camera work, which is notable primarily in the way it enhances the cinematic qualities that Gray had already built into his stage performance. In the part of *Swimming to Cambodia* where Gray mocks the parallels between movie production and government policy, he makes his points with acting techniques that demonstrate the blurred boundaries between the realms of film and politics. Gray combines the cool detachment of a politician working a crowd with the emotional intensity of a director zooming in for a closeup.

Making a movie about the bombing of Cambodia reminds Gray of demonstrations against the war in Washington and Kent State. He interrupts his description of the movie shoot to remind us that Nixon watched reruns of *Patton* while students demonstrated outside the White House. Gray flashes Nixon's famous double-V sign with upraised arms as he describes the President's midnight visit

BOOZE, CARS AND
COLLEGE GIRLS.

with the protesters. In a rapid succession of words and gestures, Gray creates a montage of images that recreate that moment in history as if it were a TV movie. Nixon on the phone asking advice from Norman Vincent Peale and Henry Kissinger. Pol Pot and the Khmer Rouge eating nuts and berries in the countryside outside Phnom Penh. General Alexander Haig declaring Cambodian President Lon Nol to be mentally unstable because he wept openly when he saw that his nation's downfall was at hand.

Gray presents this potpourri of past events with a vocal tone that suggests the objectivity of documentary realism at the same time that it hints at irony. The rhythmic pace of his story builds to a series of urgent crescendos. Every so often he stops unexpectedly, as if to reflect on the outrageous incongruities inherent in what he has just reported. The pauses encourage us to reexamine the implications of the particular image that has just passed before us, as if it were being singled out for an instant replay. Nixon, for example, inanely asking one of the student demonstrators, "How's your team doing?"

Like a good journalist, Gray uses direct quotes to help dramatize his story, but his objectivity is only an illusion. His information is factual, but his opinions seep through in the editorial shifts of his intonation and facial expression. With subdued tones of empathy and respect, Gray reads a letter from a Cambodian prince to the American ambassador refusing the offer of safe passage when the American troops withdraw from Phnom Penh. "I cannot, alas, leave in such a cowardly fashion," writes Sirik Matak. Gray dutifully reports that five days later the prince's liver was carried through the streets on a stick. Choosing that moment to take a sip of water, Gray creates a silence in which to begin his account of the Cambodian genocide. Detailing the nightmares of the "worst autogenocide in modern history," Gray hypothesizes a cloud of evil that comes down on the earth and drives men to unthinkable actions: ". . . babies torn apart like fresh bread in front of their mothers." His voice seems muted by the horror of what he describes, as if the same dark cloud were muffling his words.

Next, in an artful cinematic cut that hints at the connections between the Cambodian atrocities and the anti-Communist prejudices of individual Americans, Gray moves from the killing fields of Cambodia to an Amtrak lounge car. There he meets a Navy man who tells Gray he spends most of his time chained to a chair in a waterproof missile silo waiting for orders to push a green button that will launch a nuclear attack. Recreating his conversation with the man, Gray turns his head from side to side as he switches from the booming certainty of the sailor's militaristic anti-Russian prejudices to the incredulous confusion of Gray's stammering responses. The dialogue plays like a television talk show with Gray as the befuddled host.

Audiences accustomed to perceiving experience in electronically condensed bits of packaged information are fascinated by the compelling power of Gray's artistry. The public's interest in his technique becomes apparent when Gray performs a piece entitled *Interviewing the Audience*. He invites members of the audience onto the stage to talk about their own lives, but when they are given a chance to ask questions, they want Gray to tell them how he makes his stories so intriguing. "How do you make your life sound so interesting?" "How do you get people to say such funny things?" "How do you get people to pay attention to you for so long?" These are some of the questions Gray is asked one evening at the Brattle Theatre in Cambridge, Massachusetts.

The concerns of the audience are symptomatic of a society that has surrendered its communication skills to its television sets. Everyone wants to learn how to make their own life as funny and appealing as the monologues of their favorite celebrity talk-show host. They feel insecure about their abilities to reach out to one another through the simple exchange of conversation, and Gray offers them a model of a man talking about himself with a grace, charm and humor that draws people close to him. His style of storytelling satisfies the part of their nature that hungers for direct human contact, unmediated by technological intervention.

One of Gray's interviewees that Cambridge evening is a reporter for the *Boston Globe*. She laments the fact that she can never get people to say interesting things when she interviews them for her articles. Furthermore, she fears that she herself has nothing very interesting to say and wonders aloud whether anyone in the audience has really had a good conversation lately. A few people claim to have had satisfying discussions about movies or politics. One man said he had a good talk about reincarnation after reading about it in the *National Enquirer*. But most people seemed to agree that conversations in their personal lives left much to be desired. For both the reporter who wants to get more informative details from her interviews and average people who want more spice in their private gossip, Gray is a source of envy and inspiration.

His answers to the audience's questions are enlightening. He tells them that he develops his monologues by listening to them over and over again on tape. Each night he tapes his show, and tries to improve it, basing each new performance not on the original monologue, but on the most recent version of it. Eventually he dispenses with the tape recorder and constructs each new performance on the memory of the one that has preceded it. Ultimately his show becomes a memory of a memory of a memory of a story that has been distilled down to its essence through the process of continually being retold. Gray appears so natural on stage not because he is just being himself, but because he is so well practiced at impersonating himself as he remembers himself performing himself. This is similar to what politicians do when they make public appearances impersonating the images they have carefully cultivated to win the approval of voters. But while politicians play their roles in earnest, Gray impersonates himself with a clearly self-deprecating sense of ironic detachment.

This self-reflexive irony is the key to Gray's keen sense of humor. While the humor of a master self-performer like Ronald Reagan is calculated to lull the listeners into a reassuring state of acceptance, Gray's ironic humor is designed to encourage thoughtful reflection and critical questioning. He makes things funny by asking us to examine their credibility. In *Terrors of Pleasure* Gray plays a tape recording of a message left on his answering machine by an unscrupulous real estate salesman. The tone of Gray's voice when he introduces the recording and the expressions that pass across his face as he listens to it generate a mood of comic skepticism that makes the man's declarations of trustworthiness howlingly funny. Even more ludicrous, Gray makes clear, is the fact that he actually bought property from this man. Gray is so skilled at conveying this sense of self-mocking irony that he often casts a comic sense of doubt on his own words as he speaks them. A perfect example of a Brechtian actor, Gray has mastered the art of speaking in the first and third person simultaneously. He projects a sense of thinking about the significance of what he says, even as he is in the process of saying it.

The quality of thoughtfulness at the heart of Gray's ironic acting style makes him an undesirable candidate for typical commercial acting roles. In *Terrors of Pleasure* Gray tells the story of auditioning for a part in a television movie opposite Farrah Fawcett. The director liked him but was disturbed by something he noticed about Gray's acting in the screen test. A quality that he could only describe as "thinking" seemed to pass across Gray's face whenever he was supposed to make romantic advances towards Fawcett. That reflective quality prevented Gray from projecting the all-American "go-for-it spirit" the director was looking for, so he didn't get the role. Apparently Gray's thoughtfulness created the appearance of doubt, hesitation and ambivalence, tones that are not conducive to selling the products advertised on television, but are essential for generating the kind of disturbingly ironic humor at which Gray excels.

Gray's tones of human ambivalence are what distinguishes his memories from the mass media's versions of the past. There is an illusory objectivity to cameras and newsprint that Gray's style avoids. He may borrow the jumpcuts of cinema or the direct quotes of journalism, but he never pretends to be certain about anything. His stance is one of perpetual doubt. In *Swimming to Cambodia* he approaches the Vietnam War with a questioning tone that penetrates past the video pictures of network news and the deceptive myths of Hollywood war films. He uses these common images as a starting point, but transforms them into a kind of personalized multimedia narrative about the awakening of a political conscience. As he talks about flying up in the helicopter on location in Thailand, and describes the film producer's re-creation of dead bodies and burning villages below him, the cadences of his story accelerate markedly. His gestures pulse with the chaotic urgency of battle. There is no door on the helicopter and he is dangerously high above the ground, but he isn't afraid because he's in a movie and is comforted by the camera's power to eroticize the space it aims at. "Like Colgate Gard-All," he blurts out ridiculously, invoking the protection of an old television-commercial toothpaste shield.

Gray speaks and moves with an even greater velocity as he realizes that the movie version of the war is almost as terrifying as the real event. In a flash of intuition he comes up with the idea of "War Therapy." Countries could heal the traumas of war by reenacting it in fictional form. Gray describes his newly invented form of social healing as if it were a demented version of *The Dating Game*. Gray has lost the ability to distinguish history from the image of history he remembers in the media. He remembers seeing B-52s in the television coverage of Vietnam in the sixties but when he tries to imagine a connection between himself and the real war, Gray can only think of himself as riding a helicopter in *Apocalypse Now*. The closest association he can make to the real war is a scene from another movie.

Gray's portrayal of his frenzied condition in the helicopter gathers a breathless momentum. It is full of irony, ambivalence and mental doubletakes. The producer hopes his experience in the film will teach Gray that "morality is not a movable feast," but Gray maintains that he "sees it moving all the time." In the swirling complexity of his imagery Gray makes his audience see morality move as well. He generates a whirlwind of cross-media references that dizzy our senses. His arms move back and forth as if he is literally trying to maintain his moral equilibrium in the blur of game shows, TV commercials, film and history. His awakening conscience has to contend with a media blitz that dulls his senses into forgetting that actions have consequences that outlast the closing credits.

In *Swimming to Cambodia*, as in Gray's other monologues, there does not seem to be any source for the kind of conflict found in traditional drama. Gray's theatre is fueled by a different kind of conflict: the conflict between memory and forgetting. Remembering the real implications of war as distinct from the media's manufactured implications is crucial to Gray's awakening conscience in *Swimming to Cambodia*. The interdependence of memory and morality is central to all his work. Gray's portrayal of the struggle between individual memory and the forgetfulness induced by mass media is a potent dramatization of one of our era's most troubling dilemmas. Gray enacts this struggle each time he pulls a surprising detail out of the past and makes us believe it has just occurred to him at that moment. His stammers, his pauses, and the visible traces of thinking that pass over his face are the tangible manifestations of his unwillingness to let history slip away from him undigested. Memory is a recurring character in every one of his performances. It is pitted against the dangerous human tendency to forget the past without reflecting on its meaning.

The drama in Gray's monologues is not born out of emotional clashes. It comes from the excitement of watching him analyze, question, ridicule and embrace the details of the incidents he so artfully recalls. The audience is witnessing an intimate act in the mind of a rememberer, made visible by the power of Gray's extraordinary performance skills. They are enraptured, not because they necessarily identify with the story he is telling, but because they identify with his need to tell it. Responding to a society in which the individual is bombarded with so many images that he runs the risk of forgetting their significance, Gray stages modern morality plays, with memory as the self-reflexive hero slashing away at the dragon of mass-media oblivion. Appealing to his audience's deep collective need to remember, Gray's performance suggests the possibility of salvaging the past simply by caring enough to think about it.

From *Swimming to Cambodia*

Whenever I travel, if I have the time, I go by train. Because I like to hang out in the lounge car. I hear such great stories there—fantastic! Perhaps it's because they think they'll never see me again. It's like a big, rolling confessional.

I was on my way to Chicago from New York City when this guy came up to me and said, "Hi, I'm Jim Bean. Mind if I sit down?"

"No, I'm Spalding Gray, have a seat. What's up Jim?"

"Oh, nothing much. I'm in the Navy."

"Really? Where are you stationed?"

"Guantanamo Bay."

"Where's that?"

"Cuba."

"Really? What's it like?"

"Oh, we don't get into Cuba, man. It's totally illegal. We go down to the Virgin Islands whenever we want R & R. We get free flights down there."

"What do you do there?"

"Get laid."

"Go to whores?"

"No. I never paid for sex in my life. I get picked up by couples. I like to swing, I mean, I'm into that, you know? Threesomes, triangles, pyramids—there's power in that."

And I could see how he would be picked up. He was cute enough—insidious, but still cute. The only kind of demented thing about him was that his ears hadn't grown. They were like those little pasta shells. It was as if his body had grown but his ears hadn't caught up yet.

So I said, "Where are you off to?"

"Pittsburgh."

"Pittsburgh, my god. What's up there?"

"My wife."

"Really? How long has it been since you saw her?"

"Oh, about a year."

"I bet she's been doing some swinging herself."

"No, man, I know her. She's got fucking cobwebs growing between her legs. I wouldn't mind watching her get fucked by a guy once, no, I wouldn't mind that at all."

"Well that's quite a trip, coming from Cuba to Pittsburgh."

"No, no. I'm not stationed in Cuba anymore, man. I'm in Philly."

"Oh, well what's going on in Philly?"

"Can't tell you. No way. Top secret."

"Oh, come on, Jim. Top secret in Philadelphia? You can tell me."

"No way."

And he proceeded to have five more rum cokes and tell me that in Philadelphia he is on a battleship in a waterproof chamber, chained one arm to the wall for five hours a day, next to a green button, with earphones on. I could just see those little ears waiting for orders to fire his rockets from their waterproof silos onto the Russians. He sits there waiting with those earphones on, high on blue-flake cocaine, a new breed from Peru that he loves, with a lot of coffee because the Navy can't test for cocaine. They can test for marijuana five days after you smoke a joint, but not the cocaine. He sits there high on cocaine, chained to the wall, next to the green button, in a waterproof chamber.

"Why waterproof?" I asked. I thought I'd just start with the details and work out. I know I could have said, "Why a green button?," but it didn't matter at that point.

"Waterproof, man, because when the ship sinks and I go down to the bottom of the ocean, any ocean, anywhere, I'm still there in my waterproof chamber and I can push that green button, activate my rocket and it fires out of the waterproof silo and up, up, up it goes. I get a fucking erection every time I think of firing a rocket on those Russians. We're going to win! We're going to win this fucking war. I like the Navy, though. I fucking *like* the Navy. I get to travel everywhere. I've been to Africa, Sweden, India. I fucking didn't like Africa, though. I don't know why, but black women just don't turn me on."

Now here's a guy, if the women in the country don't turn him on, he misses the entire landscape. It's just one big fuzzball, a big black outline and he steps through to the other side of the world and comes out in Sweden.

"I fucking love Sweden, man. You get to see real Russkies in Sweden. They're marched in at gunpoint and they're only allowed two beers. We're drinking all the fucking beer we want. We're drunk on our asses, saying, 'Hey, Russkies, what's it like in Moscow this time of year?' And then we pay a couple of Swedish whores to go over and put their heads in the Russkies' laps. You should see those fuckers sweat, man. They are so stupid. We're going to win. We're going to win the fuckin' war. I mean, they are really *dumb*. They've got liquid fuel in their rockets, they're rusty and they're going to sputter, they're going to pop, they're going to land in our cornfields."

"Wait a minute, Jim. Cornfields? I mean, haven't you read the literature? It's bad enough if they land in the cornfields. We're all doomed."

"No, they're stupid. You won't believe this. The Russians don't even have electro-intercoms in their ships. They still speak through tubes!"

Suddenly I had this enormous fondness for the Russian Navy. The whole of Mother Russia. The thought of these men speaking, like innocent children, through empty toilet paper rolls, where you could still hear compassion, doubt, envy, brotherly love, ambivalence, all those human tones coming through the tube.

Jim was very patriotic. I thought it only existed on the covers of *Newsweek* and *Time*. But no, if you take the train from New York to Chicago, there it is against a pumpkin-orange sunset, Three Mile Island. Jim stood up and saluted those three big towers, then sat back down.

Meanwhile I was trying to make a mild stand. I was trying to talk him out of his ideas. I don't know what my platform was—I mean, he was standing for all of America and I was just concerned for myself at that point. I really felt as if I were looking my death in the face. I'm not making up any of these stories, I'm really not. And if *he* was making up the story he was telling me, I figure he's white, and if he wants it bad enough and he's in the Navy, if he wasn't down in that waterproof chamber then, he must be down there now.

"Jim, Jim," I said, "you don't want to do it. Remember what happened to the guy who dropped the bomb on Hiroshima? He went crazy!"

"That asshole? He was not properly brainwashed. I," he said with great pride, "have been properly brainwashed. Also there is the nuclear destruct club. Do you think I'm the only one who's going to be pressing that green button? There's a whole bunch of us going to do it."

"Wait, wait, wait. You, all of you, don't want to die, do you? You're going to die if you push that button. Think of all you have to live for." I had to think hard about this one. "The blue-flake cocaine, for instance. Getting picked up by couples. The Swedish whores. Blowing away the cobwebs between your wife's legs. I mean, really."

"No, I'm not going to die. We get 'pubs'."

Everything was abbreviated, and "pubs" meant Navy publications that tell them where to go to avoid radiation. And I could see him down there, after the rest of us have all been vaporized. He'll be down there in Tasmania or New Zealand starting this new red-faced, pea-brained, small-eared humanoid race. And I thought, the Mother needs a rest, Mother Earth needs a long, long rest.

If we're lucky he'll end up in Africa.

Anyway, he was beginning to realize that I wasn't totally on his side. It was hard to see that because I didn't have as detailed a platform as he had. Finally, he turned to me and said, "Listen Mr. Spalding," (I think by then he was calling me Gary Spalding) "you would not be doing that thing you do, writing, talking, whatever it is you do in the theatre, if it were not for me and the United States Navy stopping the Russians from taking over the world."

And I thought, wait a minute, maybe he's right. Maybe the Russians *are* trying to take over the world. Maybe *I'm* the one who's brainwashed. Maybe I've been hanging out with liberals too long. I mean, after all this time I thought I was a conscientious pacifist but maybe I've been deluding myself. Maybe I'm just a passive-aggressive unconscious coward, and like any good liberal, I should question everything. For instance, when did I last make a stand, any kind of stand, about anything? When did I just stand up for something right? Let alone America. What is America? Every time I try to think of America as a unit I get anxious. I think that's part of the reason I moved to Manhattan; I wanted to live on "an island off the coast of America." I wanted to live somewhere between America and Europe, a piece of land with very defined boundaries and only eight million people.

—*Spalding Gray*

BILL IRWIN

"The heart of clowning for me is how to get yourself into dilemmas. I don't have to look for them. They come my way."

—BILL IRWIN

Bill Irwin's baggy pants trigger a cultural memory of clowns from America's past. For silent-film stars like Buster Keaton and Charlie Chaplin oversized trousers were signs of marginality, emphasizing their inability to tailor either their clothes or their aspirations to fit society's norms. For Bill Irwin, whose comic dances express his longing to take flight from all manners of constraint, floppy trousers serve an added purpose. They are his wings. They wave, wiggle and flap as his rubber limbs dance with breezy abandon. They free his legs to keep time with the music's breathless rhythms. Watching Irwin's limbs move in dozens of directions simultaneously is like seeing Fred Astaire's body possessed by all four Marx Brothers at once. The zany grace and uncanny weightlessness of Irwin's movement convey a mood of liberation that is captured perfectly in the airy nonchalance of his billowing trousers.

But like the wings of a butterfly, Irwin's baggy pants are emblematic of a brief and fragile freedom. His blissful dances are always interrupted by sinister forces that try to bring him down to earth. In his signature comic dilemma Irwin struggles to resist an invisible vacuum that tries to suck him off the stage. Though he valiantly attempts to keep dancing, one of his legs is drawn irresistably to the wings of the proscenium, taking the rest of his body along with it. Sometimes he manages to escape, but more often than not, Irwin succumbs to the magnetic pull with a mixture of fear and resignation. As it drags him across the floor and out of the audience's view Irwin feebly tips his hat to the crowd. The perpetual frustration of Irwin's efforts to soar into soft-shoe heaven gives him the appearance of an eager vaudevillian who is forever getting the hook.

In *The Regard of Flight* Irwin's invisible nemesis is joined by a pair of human antagonists who also seem determined to prevent the clown from enjoying the pleasures of his airborne choreography. The piece, which has been performed from New York City to Los Angeles, features Doug Skinner as a pianist who doubles as a stage manager and throws Irwin off balance by giving him the music cues before he is ready. A critic, played by M.C. O'Connor, leaps out of the audience to cross-examine Irwin about the deeper implications of his work. The clown's simple desires are suffocated by the intrusive blare of the stage manager's warning signal and the nasal drone of the critic's pretentious questions. The more Irwin tries to resist, the more relentlessly they pursue him. With trampolines and loudspeakers to assist them, Irwin's adversaries try to impose their ideas on him, but he refuses to give up his dreams of theatrical flight. His pursuers, however, are equally persistent, chasing Irwin through the audience as well as around the stage. The critic suddenly becomes a director and forces Irwin to act Shakespeare in his pajamas. The pianist manages to sneak his ventriloquist act into the show. And all along the unseen force is waiting in the wings to suck Irwin offstage the moment he starts dancing.

In spite of these difficulties, Irwin continues to fight back. He shoots the piano player and stabs the journalistic vampire through the heart with a giant pencil. Irwin's resourcefulness does not give him a total victory, but it does provide him with a few short opportunities to dance. These moments never last much longer than a minute; it is precisely their fragmentary and elusive quality that makes them so evocative. Irwin's solo dances linger in the memory as unfinished visual poems in which the spirit of freedom is personifed by a bumbling clown in baggy pants who wants nothing more than a chance to dance his way to the clouds. Irwin's mastery of his body seems perfect enough to lift him into flight, and there is even a segment where he appears on a platform over the audience's heads, flapping his arms and threatening to jump into the void. It is an exhilarating moment, as Irwin almost convinces the audience that he can fly if he wants to, but the critic talks him out of it, clipping the clown's wings with intellectual jargon and specious logic. Their exchange epitomizes the ongoing tension between the clown who longs to break free from the restraints of reason and gravity, and the mundane forces that prevent him from taking flight.

It is Irwin's physical skills that give him the ability to meet each new threat with such remarkable resilience. No matter how many times the menacing proscenium

pulls him off the stage, he always reemerges ready to perform another astonishing feat of terpsichorean acrobatics. When the critic belittles his talents with derogatory questions about "hat tricks," Irwin responds by dropping his hat and executing a full front flip that miraculously finishes with the hat on his head. Following the stage manager's long-winded speech about the way in which "new theatre" demystifies drama by presenting costume changes in full view of the audience, Irwin puts his vest on backwards and upside down. He triumphs over both the vest and the tedious introduction with a dazzling double arm reversal that puts his vest right side up without his having to remove it.

Irwin's physical virtuosity wins the respect of the audience, but the attitude with which he presents his skills is what makes him funny. Undermining his talents with self-deprecating remarks about his insecurities, Irwin adds a modernizing twist of irony to old-fashioned slapstick routines. In *The Regard of Flight* the battle between the clown dancer and his wacky antagonists is set in the context of an avant-garde burlesque show. Irwin is not only trying to dance. He is trying to realize his vision of a "new theatre" that rejects the "cheap devices" and "empty polish" of the "bourgeois theatre." But at the same time that he is trying to create something new, he is sentimentally attached to the baggage of traditional clowning. He denounces the deceitful tricks of conventional theatre, but he can't resist the temptation to pull a rabbit out of a hat from his old trunk of props. As soon as the audience responds sentimentally to the furry creature, Irwin undercuts their reaction by revealing that the "bunny" is a fake. With episodes like this Irwin is shifting back and forth between two realms of theatre, getting visceral laughs with traditional gags and intellectual laughs by ironically dissecting them.

The pattern is set up early in the show when Irwin makes the crowd guffaw by leaning forward at an impossible angle with no visible means of support. This stunt is followed by a drily comic monologue in which the stage manager discusses the disadvantages of the lean-shoe device used to achieve the "cantilever effect." Irwin uses the lean shoes again when he appears high above the audience's heads and announces his intentions to fly away from the limitations of the bourgeois theatre. Like that moment of self-referential suspension when the clown's feet are bound by an old circus contraption while the rest of his body reaches recklessly into the realm of postmodern free-fall, Irwin's entire performance teeters ironically on the edge between conventional and contemporary forms of comedy. He draws the audience into an innocent involvement with a naive clown at the same time that he entices them into a more sophisticated entanglement with a self-mocking experimentalist.

The multileveled structure of *Regard of Flight* reflects the diversity of Irwin's background. In the early seventies he immersed himself in the self-conscious experiments of avant-garde theatre as a member of Herbert Blau's KRAKEN ensemble. He developed his dance skills during the same period through occasional performances with the Oberlin Dance Collective. This experimental work did not satisfy Irwin's desire to make direct contact with the audience in a lighter key, so he enrolled in the Ringling Brothers Clown College in 1974 and spent five years as a traditional white-faced clown with San Francisco's Pickle Family Circus (1976-81). When Irwin left the circus and began creating work for the stage in San Francisco and New York, his experimental impulses merged with his love for popular entertainment in pieces like *The Regard of Flight*. His unique combination of talents won him the praise of critics on both coasts, numerous television appearances, and a slew of prestigious awards including an Obie and a five-year MacArthur "genius grant," the first to go to a performing artist.

Having established his credentials as both a popular entertainer and an experimental innovator, Irwin began exploring still another area of theatre that added new textures to his performance. Social satire is an implicit element in *The Regard of Flight*, which includes pointed parodies of the avant-garde, but the satirical side of Irwin's clowning emerged more explicitly after his experience acting in the work of the Italian political satirist Dario Fo. In 1984 Irwin appeared in the Broadway production of Fo's *Accidental Death of an Anarchist*. His role was small, but he had the opportunity to meet Fo during the run, and was left with a lasting respect for the playwright's sharp and specific sense of political humor. The next spring, New York's Music-Theatre Group produced an Irwin work-in-progress entitled *The Courtroom*, which attempted to integrate physical comedy and political satire in the context of nonlinear experimental theatre. His collaborators in this experiment included juggler Michael Moschen, clown Bob Berky, puppet-maker Julie Taymor and breakdancer Rory Mitchell.

The Courtroom depicts the dilemma of a man who goes into a courthouse to apply for a bicycle license and ends up enmeshed in an impenetrable web of legal bureaucracy. Irwin's innocent victim is overwhelmed by the imposing size and grandeur of the courtroom, which seems designed to reduce the defendant to physical insignificance. Again it is his dancing that gives Irwin the power to assert himself. He is hesitant at first, but eventually he makes his case to the judge through a dance routine with a top hat and cane. The prosecuting attorney answers with a dance of his own, and the stenographer plays it back for the judge in the form of a tap dance. This is a courtroom in which motions are introduced by people who really know how to move. Another series of motions is introduced to the courtroom by a team of lawyers who turn out to be break dancers. He is also baffled by evidence presented as juggling balls. Lawyers and witnesses flip the balls as nimbly as they toss off legal terminology. The juggling patterns shift and reverse, as if we were watching facts being manipulated and information being rearranged. Deliberately intended to dazzle, bewilder and intimidate the defendant, the jugglers' routines are the visual equivalent of legal rhetoric and argumentation.

Irwin's courtroom is a battleground that represents the flaws of the American legal system with vivid physical metaphors. The interested parties are trying to outmaneuver one another with shrewd strategies. Skill is power, and the court is overflowing with flashy performers, eager to display their talents to give themselves a competitive edge. Justice and truth are sacrificed to showmanship, and

Irwin's innocent character is lost in the razzle-dazzle of the spectacle that rages around him. It is only during the recess that he is able to gather his energies for another attempt to make his point through a simple honest dance. Discovering that the court records are the kind you can play on a phonograph, he choreographs a few steps to their music while the courtroom is empty. With no one around to disrupt his train of thought, Irwin does a beautiful solo. It is as balanced, relaxed and self-assured as an airtight argument. He directs his dance to the jury box, as if to persuade the nonexistent jurors that everything can be explained with ease. His limbs move through space with the confidence and clarity of irrefutable logic. He controls his body, his cane and his hat with the smooth grace of a man in complete command of the situation at hand. When people begin filing back into the courtroom, we anticipate a scene in which truth will triumph over chicanery, but the presence of an audience shakes Irwin's confidence. The stress of social pressure distorts the truth as he was prepared to tell it, and he loses control of his body. His legs quiver. His thighs tremble. His head jerks. The courtroom erupts into chaos, in sharp contrast to the calm mood of reason that prevailed when Irwin was alone. The scales of justice tilt when the dancer loses his balance.

After his ambitious experiments in *The Courtroom*, Irwin tackled the demanding role of Galy Gay in Bertolt Brecht's political comedy *A Man's a Man*. The play was directed by Robert Woodruff at the La Jolla Playhouse in California. Like the protagonist in *The Courtroom*, Galy Gay is an innocent victim caught in a web of spiraling complications. A dockworker who goes out to buy a fish for dinner and gets hoodwinked into enlisting in the army, Galy Gay is transformed from a docile man into a killer. In a black comedy where the stakes are high, Irwin's physical skills are linked to his character's survival in the face of death.

In a trial scene as comically absurd as Irwin's own *Courtroom*, Galy Gay is threatened with execution on trumped-up charges that he was involved in the fraudulent sale of a fake elephant. The soldiers who stage the mock prosecution are trying to convince Galy Gay to take another man's name. The verdict is guilty and Galy Gay faces a firing squad. When Irwin takes a pratfall, there is a silence, followed by the laughter that comes with the audience's realization that Galy Gay's fear, not the phony bullets, brought him to the ground. When he regains consciousness, he is confronted with a coffin containing what he is told is the body of Galy Gay. Ordered to agree that he is dead or to take another man's name, Irwin physicalizes his dilemma with a variation of his signature clown routine. He is mysteriously drawn to the coffin by the same kind of force that usually drags him off the stage. As he tries to resist the coffin's magnetic pull he speaks Brecht's fragmented monologue: "If I looked, I'd fall dead. A face emptied out into a crate. Someone looked in the water and saw that face in the shimmering surface of the water, and did drop dead; I can vouch for that. So how could I open this crate? I'm afraid. And who am I? I am a Both: there are two of me."

The presence of a menacing double that threatens the protagonist's identity links Brecht's text to recurring themes in Irwin's clowning. In *Regard of Flight* the critic dresses himself up in a baggy-pants clown costume identical to Irwin's own, and proceeds to imitate Irwin's dancing. At one point in the play Irwin is chased around in circles by the double, who criticizes him with comments that echo Irwin's own self-conscious concerns about the validity of the "new theatre." Irwin is being pursued by a phantom of himself, a material embodiment of his fears. The same disturbing combination of slapstick anxiety and double identity is employed by Irwin in *Not Quite New York*, performed at New York's Dance Theater Workshop in 1981. In both works Irwin trips repeatedly over a nonexistent bump as he tries to escape from his double. When he finally manages to anticipate the obstacle and leap over it, still another invisible bump lands him flat on his face. The pratfall connects the clown's precarious sense of balance to his precarious sense of self.

Another way in which Irwin's aesthetics overlap with those of Brecht is in the acting style. Irwin's own creations constantly require him to act his role as he

BILL IRWIN AS GALY GAY IN THE LA JOLLA PLAYHOUSE PRODUCTION OF <u>A MAN'S A MAN</u>.

comments on it, so he can readily grasp Brecht's concept of *Verfremdungseffekt*, which asks actors to perform in first and third person simultaneously. It is not coincidental that Irwin's style meshes so smoothly with Brecht's. The German playwright was deeply influenced by popular entertainment traditions, and counted the German music-hall clown Karl Valentin as one of his most important teachers. (In the lobby of the La Jolla Playhouse when Irwin performed *A Man's a Man* there was a blown-up photograph of Brecht playing the clarinet in a clown piece directed by Valentin.) Irwin's early training in experimental theatre exposed him to Brecht's techniques even before he became a clown. In KRAKEN's theatri-

cal exploration of cannibalism, Irwin added a note of black humor by repeating a death scene over and over. The slapstick fall he used in that macabre piece of experimental humor was the same fall he ended up using for Galy Gay's collapse in front of the firing squad almost fifteen years later.

Irwin's attraction to both Brecht and the experimental work of KRAKEN was rooted in his desire to make a deep and direct connection with the audience. Brecht advocated *Verfremdungseffekt* as a way of insuring the spectator's active mental participation in the performance and many of KRAKEN's exercises were designed to facilitate a similar kind of direct interaction. But it was in the Pickle

Family Circus that Irwin had his first extended opportunity to develop his instinctual ability to create a sense of intimacy between himself and the public. Brecht and the KRAKEN group had also appealed to Irwin's interest in nonnaturalistic performance rather than emotional realism as a means of connecting to the audience. Spinning plates and juggling hats as Willy the Clown in the circus, Irwin perfected the difficult skill of making real bonds with the audience while engaged in surreal acts.

In one of Willy's most popular circus routines, carried over into the series of "Bagatelles" performed as a coda to *Regard of Flight,* Irwin portrays a hapless waiter in an Italian restaurant. Willy's only adversary is a pot of spaghetti with a mind of its own. He begins his efforts to take charge by deftly manipulating a plate, flipping it from his elbow to his hand with an eloquence that surprises even himself. From the beginning Irwin uses his absurd relationship with the plate to win the audience's respect and woo their applause, so that they are on his side when he engages in comic combat with the spaghetti. With a fork as his only weapon, Willy drops, stabs, swirls, spins and discards three platefuls of pasta. The pasta seems to be endowed with a stubbornness beyond what is to be expected from an ordinary plate of spaghetti, and Willy rises to the challenge by wrestling the food onto his plate with gravity-defying feats of finesse. Irwin himself never leaves the ground but he creates the illusion that his spaghetti has wings, and he makes the audience feel like his silent partner in a ridiculous conspiracy to make the pasta fly onto his plate. It is the same subtle and unspoken bond that Irwin creates with the public each time he dances a step that hints at the possibility of sending his body into flight. The pure delight in watching Irwin's clown break into a rubber-limbed softshoe is related to the pleasure of seeing him twirl globs of phony spaghetti on a fork. Both enable the audience to participate in the accomplishment of the seemingly impossible.

Maintaining a state of freedom is a frequent theme in Irwin's career choices as well as in his routines. He joined Herbert Blau's experimental theatre ensemble to avoid being trapped behind the fourth wall of traditional acting. Then he signed up with the circus to escape the insular elitism of the avant-garde. But the circus ring had its own limitations, so Irwin moved on to the creation of his unique clown-theatre pieces. Now that he has won mainstream acceptance for his work, Irwin is beginning to receive offers to appear in film and television, and he is trying to avoid the pitfalls of popular success in a culture where the arts are swallowed up by the mass media. He is intrigued by the possibilites that working in new media would open up for him, but he is wary of losing his artistic autonomy to the goblins of technology. These ambivalent feelings were evident in Irwin's first original work for television—the American Place Theater production of *Regard of Flight* was videotaped for Public Television's Great Performances series— which tells the story of a dancer who gets mysteriously trapped inside a television set while waiting for an audition.

Irwin's television nightmare was commissioned by the PBS *Live from Off Center* series and created in collaboration with video artist Charles Atlas. Entitled *As Seen on TV*, the program follows the misadventures of an aspiring hoofer (Irwin) who is literally sucked into a video monitor in a casting-office waiting room. Irwin tries to resist the pull of the tube, much as his stage persona tries to resist the offstage force that pulls him into the wings, but in the process of trying to escape, he falls out a window and climbs back in to find himself trapped inside the video screen on which the accident was recorded. To further complicate the situation, a trained monkey, who is also waiting for an audition, grabs the television's remote-control device. Each time he changes the channel, Irwin is thrown into a new video environment.

The comic illusion is similar to the one invented by Buster Keaton in *Sherlock Junior*, where a movie-theatre projectionist dreams himself onto the screen and gets caught in a series of visual non sequiturs as the scenes change from doorsteps to waterfalls to city street curbs. Irwin's modern variation of the gag sends him to a soap opera, a musical production number, and a B-movie rerun. At one point he appears in an animated alphabet sequence being watched by two puppets. He leaps out of the screen only to discover that the puppets are characters on *Sesame Street* and he is still stuck in TV.

As Seen on TV is inventive and well executed, but ultimately unsatisfying. The program diminishes the performance skills that make Irwin unique by relying heavily on camera tricks and special effects. The scenario never calls for Irwin to do anything that couldn't be done by an ordinary actor. His special talents for outwitting gravity are lost in a weightless electronic medium. Epitomizing the problem that it satirizes, the video actually does swallow up Irwin's performance identity.

Interestingly, these flaws disappeared when Irwin adapted the scenario for the theatre. Alone on stage with a video monitor and camera, Irwin still comes out on the losing end of the battle against technology, but the vulnerability of the live performer is more compelling, and the virtuosity with which he tries to defend himself raises the struggle to the level of high art. The clown eyes the camera with suspicion, and his wariness is captured immediately on the monitor positioned to face the audience. All the nuances of his mistrust are relayed to the audience in duplicate, and when Irwin begins wrestling ineptly with a tripod his awkwardness is captured immediately on the screen as well. The audience laughs at both the clown's bumbling and the echo of his reactions as recorded on the face of his electronic double. Irwin's legs get tangled up in the camera cord so that the tripod's legs and his own become almost indistinguishable. Frenetically playing out the steps of his strange five-legged duet, the clown eventually succeeds in dismantling the tripod, but the camera takes its revenge by publicly documenting all his facial twitches of fear and insecurity.

Eventually Irwin manages to remove the camera from the stage, but when he turns towards the monitor, he discovers he cannot resist its pull. As his body parts pass behind the machine they appear miraculously enlarged on the screen, as if the TV set were a magnifying glass of his imperfections. The routine ends with a startling image—Irwin's terrified face is captured on the screen and freezes into an electronic portrait of fear as the lights go out and the curtains close. Getting sucked into the video tube is the technological equivalent of being sucked off the stage. Both dilemmas are slapstick expressions of the tenacity with which the clown is able to survive in the face of annihilation.

In the end Irwin always manages to do more than just survive. Whether he is battling pretentious critics, resisting the pull of technology or taming a plateful of wild pasta, Irwin keeps his dignity as well as his body intact. His frustrated desires to fly express the dreams and fears of his audience in surreal passages of inspired buffoonery. Using aspirations for the impossible as fuel for slapstick, he is like Icarus with baggy pants, laughing at his melting wings as he prepares for a pratfall and thumbs his nose at the sun.

From *Regard of Flight*

The critic (Michael O'Connor) who has been chasing Irwin corners him in a trunk and begins questioning him. The audience sees only Irwin's head sticking out of the trunk.

CRITIC: You know we've had a lot of the imagery and so forth, and well it might be nice if we tried to sort of tie it all together at this point. First there was this guy dancing, and then—

IRWIN: Me, I was dancing.

CRITIC: Oh, well you can't be both John the Baptist and the one who danced before the king.

IRWIN: Well I'm not John the Baptist.

CRITIC: Well, as soon as I saw your head here, that's what I got, I mean I got John the Baptist. Now are you saying you're not?

IRWIN: Well, my head is here because—

CRITIC: Just answer yes or no.

IRWIN: Well, then no. I don't intend—

CRITIC: You may step down.

Irwin turns and his head disappears into the trunk, as he mimes walking down flights of steps.

CRITIC: Okay, so you're a prophet.

IRWIN: No, nonprofit.

CRITIC: Well, what was that stuff earlier, something about aspect of prophecy?

IRWIN: Oh well at that point I was speaking metaphorically.

CRITIC: Ah, metaphor. What's the central metaphor?

IRWIN: Of this work?

CRITIC: Well I guess it's martyrdom, isn't it. I mean, John the Baptist—

IRWIN: I am not John the Baptist.

CRITIC: You don't mean you're the other one?

IRWIN: What other one?

CRITIC: The one who came after. I think that's a bit much.

IRWIN: No, I'm not the other one. You see, it's modern. I'm not anyone.

CRITIC: You may step down.

Irwin turns, mimes walking down flights of steps, and disappears into the trunk.

CRITIC: Okay, you said you were dancing before.

IRWIN: That's right, I was.

CRITIC: Before who?

IRWIN: Before you were asking these questions.

CRITIC: No, no, no, no, no. Before the king. Don't you see? We have to tie all this in with John the Baptist.

IRWIN: I am not John the Baptist.

CRITIC: All right, forget John the Baptist. We still have a king. We still have a martyr. Well, let's just say you're Saint Thomas.

IRWIN: No, I am not Saint Thomas.

CRITIC: Well, then you may step down.

Irwin looks down apprehensively into the trunk.

IRWIN: Well, what if I said I was Saint Thomas?

CRITIC: Okay.

IRWIN: Okay.

CRITIC: All right.

IRWIN: Okay.

CRITIC: Fine.

IRWIN: You can see whatever you want to see. I would just like to get out of the trunk.

CRITIC: Fine, fine. We'll put you down as Saint Thomas à Becket.

IRWIN: A Becket. You didn't say Beckett?

CRITIC: Well that's who you are. You just agreed.

IRWIN: Well, yeah, but that sounds like Samuel Beckett.

CRITIC: Yes, it certainly does.

IRWIN: My work. I mean, you think what I do is like Samuel Beckett. Is this—

CRITIC: Well, yes. The offstage forces. This whole fixation with the New Testament.

IRWIN: Dances. Ukulele. How about that? That's not Samuel Beckett.

CRITIC: What are you talking about?

IRWIN: I'm talking about—

CRITIC: That's irrelevant.

The critic pushes Irwin into the trunk and slams the lid shut.

—"The Trunk Dialogue" by
Bill Irwin, in collaboration with
Doug Skinner and Michael
O'Connor

PENN & TELLER

"If I say to you as every mentalist since the beginning of time has said: 'I can read your mind—I'm going to hold these cards up, you're going to pull one out, and then, psychically, using powers everybody has, that I've developed more, I'm going to tell you what that card is,' there's a lot going on there. One thing is you've got a chip on your shoulder, and you don't believe me. The second is that I'm insulting your intelligence. And the third thing is that I've got a hook that is old and doesn't fly. You've seen it a thousand times. Now if on the other hand I come out, I fan that deck of cards, and I say to you: 'Bullshit. There's no fucking ESP. I'm not reading your fucking mind. I learn to do shit to be able to fuck with you in ways you ain't been fucked with before. And I'm going to tell you what that card is, and I'm going to tell you something else—I don't got nothing. I don't got nothing but the fact that I'm going to cheat you, and I'm going to dick you around, and I'm going to yank you, until I know what that fucking card is.' Now which one of these has more social and political repercussions."

—PENN JILLETTE

The Broadway playbill for *Penn & Teller* includes a credit for Director of Covert Activities. The ironic reference to the Iran/contra affair provides an appropriate introduction to a show that revolves around the perpetration of cover-ups. Traditional magicians call themselves illusionists. Penn and Teller call themselves swindlers. Openly acknowledging that deception is essential to the art of stage magic, they announce their fraudulent intentions from the start. Any magician can astonish an audience with sleight of hand. Penn and Teller prefer sleight of mind. As they are engaged in the process of misleading us, they reveal their methods of misdirection, but shrewdly withhold just enough information to hoodwink us in the end. Their tantalizing technique of partial revelation turns the performance into an intellectual striptease that mirrors the structure of a Congressional investigation by peeling away layers of illusion while stopping short of full disclosure. We know we shouldn't trust them, but they manage to fool us all the same. In the age of Ronald Reagan, Ed Meese and Oliver North, Penn and Teller offer a cautionary entertainment that reveals the extent of our national gullibility.

Challenging the audience to approach their material with an attitude of comic skepticism, Penn and Teller open their stage show with a hoax: a zany piece of sadomasochistic escape artistry masquerading as a poetry reading. The tall, overbearing Penn Jillette introduces the routine in a raspy voice that resonates with multiple levels of irony. He asks the audience to help him prepare for his literary presentation by binding his partner Teller in a straitjacket. Short and fragile-looking, Teller says nothing as Penn encourages the volunteers to pull the straps as tightly as possible, but he communicates his suffering clearly through the weary resignation in his face. If Penn and Teller were street hustlers, Teller would be the one who grabbed your sympathy while Penn grabbed your wallet.

The outrageous routine that ensues combines sham and virtuosity in perfect proportion. The straitjacketed Teller is hung upside down over a bed of nails, suspended from a rope that is tied to the chair on which Penn sits as he reads

PENN JILLETTE AND
TELLER.

"Casey at the Bat." He has announced that he will stand up and take a bow at the conclusion of the poem, an action which will release the rope and send Teller head first into the nails. Penn begins to read with a nonchalance that contrasts sharply with the urgent gestures of his partner, trying to wriggle out of the jacket before the poem's conclusion. Houdini pitted his skills as an escape artist against the forces of nature and technology. Penn and Teller choose instead to mine the dramatic potential of bad poetry. The suspense builds as the banal rhyming patterns roll off Penn's lips. He milks the situation for laughs by speeding up his reading as he gets closer to the end, eliciting frantic spasms from his inverted partner. When Teller finally extricates himself seconds before Penn finishes the poem, the audience responds with an intriguing blend of cheers, laughter and thought. They are expressing admiration for Teller's formidable skills as an escape artist and relief that he has survived his dilemma, but these overt reactions are mixed with a subtler appreciation of the ingenious way in which the fraud was executed.

Penn and Teller are expert confidence men, and their sadomasochistic poetry reading is the opening step of a complex relationship that the overbearing Penn and the silent Teller will continue to develop with their audience. Everyone knows that Penn is not going to let his partner fall on the nails and die, and Penn knows that everyone knows, but he plays out the charade convincingly enough to generate genuine suspense. Penn's self-consciously bombastic acting style is a rhetorical mask that allows him to parody his own callous cynicism at the same time that he carries it to the edge of believability. He used the same device in an even more extreme form on *Saturday Night Live* when he pretended to allow Teller to drown in a tank of water. "My partner is dead," he announced to the national television audience with the breezy tone of a talk-show host saying goodbye to one of his guests. This type of gallows humor is typical of Penn and Teller's style; the water-tank routine was incorporated into their Broadway stage show. Pain and death are among the duo's favorite comic illusions. The title of their forthcoming feature film is *Penn & Teller Get Killed*.

The pair's show-business background is as unconventional as their performance. Teller—even offstage he goes by this single name—was a high school Latin teacher moonlighting as a magician when Penn first saw him perform in the mid-seventies. Working with a musician, they toured the country in a show called *The Asparagus County Cultural Society* that eventually evolved into *Penn & Teller*, which won them an Obie award and was later remodeled for a successful Broadway run in the 1987-88 season. Penn Jillette and juggler Michael Moschen, who attended the same high school in Greenfield, Massachusetts, began performing together as teenagers. Penn is a 1973 graduate of the Ringling Brothers Clown College who could never reconcile his esoteric clown routines with the mainstream needs of the circus. One of his most memorable performances at the college was "The Caribou Gag," in which he appeared in the circus ring wearing antlers lit up with Christmas-tree bulbs. There was no plot or action to the routine, but it was an early indication of the bizarre comic talent that emerged in his later collaboration with Teller.

Although friendship is one of the unspoken themes of their show, Penn and Teller do not shrink from violent impulses. Their onstage relationship vacillates from hostile to compassionate, and forms another complex element in their rapport with the audience. At times Penn will turn on his partner and criticize the way he is manipulating the audience. Interrupting a card trick, Penn informs an audience volunteer that Teller has forced a card on her. He chastises Teller for resorting to such a cheap trick, and warns the audience not to let themselves be deceived by Teller's second-rate theatrics. Penn humiliates his partner with increasingly obnoxious insults, including a put-down of card tricks as inherently wimpy. Teller says nothing to defend himself, but glares at Penn with silent rage. When the tension between them has built up to an uncomfortable level of mutual loathing, Teller suddenly plunges a dagger into Penn's hand. There is a scream

and a moment of terror, until the audience notices that the card Teller has been looking for is impaled on the dagger in Penn's palm, dripping with stage blood. The fraud is executed with consummate skill. As one hoax is being uncovered, another is being engineered. In the end Penn undercuts everything he has led us to believe by announcing that he would never side with the audience against his partner.

This multileveled interplay between sham and revelation is repeated thoughout the show, alerting the audience to the constant possibility of deceit, and encouraging intellectual involvement as the public tries to discern the illusion from the truth. Unlike traditional stage magicians who try to make their illusions seem effortless, Penn and Teller create intentional wrinkles in their tricks to engage the audience in the process of trying to figure out how they are being deceived. Their method recalls the techniques of P.T. Barnum, who lured millions to his fraudulent exhibits in the nineteenth century by creatively planting doubts in the public mind about their authenticity. Barnum is remembered as the man who said, "There's a sucker born every minute," but he did not underestimate the intelligence of his customers. When he exhibited curiosities like the FeeJee mermaid and George Washington's 140-year-old nanny (advertised as "the first woman to put pants on the father of our country"), Barnum mounted sophisticated publicity campaigns that always included denunciations of the exhibits as hoaxes. He planted an anonymous newspaper story which explained that George Washington's nanny was actually a cleverly constructed automaton made of whalebone and India rubber. This strategy intrigued even the people who had already seen the exhibition, and led them to return to try and figure out how they had been fooled.

Penn and Teller play on the public's fascination with deceit in a similar way, adding an element of ironic humor to their intellectual showmanship. Twentieth-century heirs to Barnum's humbuggery, Penn and Teller devise their performances as a series of cognitive brain twisters that dare the audience to uncover their methods of trickery. Once the crowd is caught up in the mental puzzle-solving, the performers evoke laughter by presenting blatantly transparent illusions, like "Mofo, the psychic gorilla." Mofo is a fake gorilla head attached to an elaborate contraption of tubes and flashing lights. Penn and Teller satirize conventional mindreading acts by making Mofo so phony that not even a child could miss the obvious fact that Mofo's voice is really Teller speaking through a microphone. While the audience laughs at the obvious fakery of the gorilla, and smiles at the violation of the pretense that Teller can't talk, they are still baffled by Teller's ability to answer questions about which he has no information. Again, the comic revelation of sham coexists with the skilled exhibition of fraud.

Penn and Teller never condescend to their audiences by pretending that their magic is real. Instead they present themselves as shameless charlatans, and win our respect for the skill which enables them to fool us even after we've been informed that we're being fooled. Their unique method of presenting the well-known cups and balls illusion is emblematic of their approach. First they perform the traditional version in which tinfoil balls seem to defy logic by appearing and disappearing under three cups being manipulated by the performers. Then they repeat the same trick with clear plastic cups so that the audience can see how the balls are being palmed and substituted during the routine. The second time through is more entertaining than the first because the audience can't keep up with the action even though the deception is being dissected step by step as it is being perpetrated. The illusion is demystified, but the skill of misdirection acquires a mystique of its own.

Acts like these are emblems of American consumerism, where misdirection flourishes as a widely accepted business technique. Mass-media advertisements deemphasize the flaws of products while highlighting attributes that have nothing to do with their value. Cigarette health warnings are written in small print so that the buyers' attention will be attracted by the illusion of rugged masculinity or sexual pleasure that is being hawked as a fringe benefit of smoking. Advertising is just a sophisticated version of the cups and balls routine, and watching the stunt performed with clear plastic cups is like being invited into an advertising-agency planning session. Penn and Teller invite you to watch the mechanisms that are being used to deceive you, to look at the features of the trick that are normally hidden from view. They distinguish themselves from other hucksters by their willingness to admit that they are swindlers, and their determination to make their self-incrimination as entertaining as possible.

The performance encourages the audience to question everything they see. Did that really happen? Was it a trick? How did they do it? Am I too naive? Penn's running monologue stimulates these questions by referring self-consciously to the illusions as he and Teller perform them. When he stops Teller's card trick to ask the volunteer whether she chose the card of her own free will, Penn introduces the concept of a "force," explaining that a skilled performer can "force" you to pick the card he wants you to pick, and make you believe you chose it on your own. He returns to the theme throughout the evening, comically pointing out how easy it is to be manipulated, and connecting misdirection on the stage to misdirection in other spheres of life. When a man insists that he has made a free choice, Penn mocks his innocence. "You must have loved the last election," he barks.

Penn and Teller's cheerful cynicism is an antidote to consumer fraud. Their madcap hoaxes call attention to the many methods by which shams are perpetrated. In the fast-talking carnivalesque conclusion to the first half of their stage show they engage the audience in dart-throwing, crap-shooting, and other forms of rambunctious behavior to generate a randomly selected passage from the Bible. As Penn is soliciting numbers for the book, chapter and verse to be read, he keeps questioning audience members about the role of fate, skill, chance and free will in their choices. His spiel is so dizzying in its changing points of reference that the Bible passage he finds himself reading at the end seems charged with supernatural potency. Although there is no way its choice could have been forced, when Teller smashes open a glass jar that had been sealed at the beginning of the show, he reveals that the passage is written on the paper inside. After all the cautions about deception, Penn and Teller have managed to fool the audience yet again. The crowd is baffled, but Penn is quick to debunk the magic. "It's just a trick," he says as he mingles with the audience during intermission. "And if I say anything else about it, I'll only deliberately mislead you."

Penn's rapport with the audience during intermission is a continuation of the relationship he has developed with them during the performance. He speaks to them directly, without pretense. He is not playing a role, he is simply explaining the facts. Penn continues to refer to the tricks with irony, implying that both he and the audience are aware that it's all part of show business. As in the performance, the ironic attitude brings the audience closer to him. Interestingly, Penn's loud and mildly abrasive stage presence is tempered with compassion. He mocks ignorance so that people won't let themselves be taken for suckers, and there is poignance to his hard-edged approach. In spite of the fact that Penn spits chewed apples at the audience, everything he says makes clear that he respects their intelligence.

By the time the stage show draws to a close, Penn has stopped shouting and running through the theatre aisles. He has achieved an intimacy with the audience that enables him to speak to them softly, in an almost confessional tone. Sitting peacefully on a stool, he talks about sideshows and his infatuation with carnival freaks, especially "self-made freaks" like the fire-eaters. Penn's monologue resonates with earlier segments of the performance in which he and Teller twist the ordinary into the bizarre, sometimes mocking themselves, but never completely deflating the mystery of what they do. Teller's needle-swallowing act, for instance, is an excruciatingly perverse and sublimely executed example of the duo's postmodern sideshow technique. He slowly sucks each needle down his throat, pausing long enough for the audience to imagine the sensations that he might be experiencing. Then Teller gulps and winces in a silent exhibition of suffering that culminates in his pulling the needles out of his stomach threaded on a string. The

audience knows it is a trick, but they have been swindled with such dignity that they can only stare in awe, like country bumpkins in a sideshow tent.

Penn confirms the public's feelings of carnival voyeurism in his closing monologue. "You're in our tent," he says, playing on the unsettling moods that have been building all through the show. His ostensible subject is the art of fire-eating, but he's really talking about the art of performance, the obsession to display oneself in public, the fragile quality of the connection between an actor and his audience, and the human need for mystery. He dissects the techniques of fire-eating as he speaks, and concludes with a demonstration of the art. As is true with the cups and balls routine, the explanation does not diminish the impact of the event itself. Penn's discussion only serves to heighten the meanings we project onto the act of extinguishing flames in one's mouth.

Fire-eaters, illusionists, escape artists and cardsharps, Penn and Teller are consummate American hucksters. Each of their routines is a complex package of skill, sham, irony and showmanship. They are virtuosic con men, who orchestrate their physical comedy into poetic emblems of American gullibility. Their comic fraudulence is rooted in America's preoccupation with success. Confidence men can exist only in a culture that believes in miracles. They feed on their victims' hope for the impossible: a miracle cure, a foolproof road to riches, the fountain of youth. "Casey at the Bat" is a national classic because it aches with the "hope eternal" that Casey can beat the odds and save the game with a home run in the bottom of the ninth. Casey always strikes out, but the fans in Mudville never give up until the final empty swing of the bat. Teller's escape from the straitjacket becomes the longshot equivalent of Casey's grand slam, and when he manages to wriggle free just in time, the audience cheers like the fans in Mudville would cheer if Casey hadn't let them down.

Penn and Teller have devised the perfect entertainment for a nation overrun with cover-ups, covert operations, and deceptive advertising campaigns. They swindle their audience with integrity, transparently deceiving them with comic hoaxes that sharpen their sensitivity to the sales pitches they'll inevitably encounter when they leave the theatre. (The first one comes when they find Penn selling "Mofo - The Psychic Gorilla" T-shirts in the lobby.) Teller's ability to avoid being impaled on the bed of nails is simple compared with what it takes to escape the misleading traps of business and politics in America. Penn and Teller's comic sideshow offers a crash course in the survival skills of a consumer democracy. While the audience members may not be transformed from suckers to skeptics overnight, they might be a little more prone to laugh the next time a politician or salesman tells them there's nothing up his sleeve.

From *Penn & Teller*

The stage is dark. Penn speaks to the audience.

Everything that Teller and I do in this show comes from a love that we share of the American sideshow, the freak show.

Penn lights a candle. He is seated on a stool.

Now, the real name for the freak show is the Ten-in-One Show, and it's called the Ten-in-One Show because you get ten acts under one tent for one admission price.

When I was a kid I used to go to the Franklin County Fair—that's where the carnival came in my hometown. And that fair would be in town about ten days every year, and every one of those ten days I'd go to the fair, and every day at the fair, I'd wind up at the Ten-in-One Show. And I loved the freak show. I loved it because you'd pay your seventy-five cents and you were allowed to go into a tent with people who were entirely different from you, and then you could just stare at them.

And I loved the freaks, but I especially loved the self-made freaks, the fire-eater, the sword swallower, the tattooed people, because they had made an extra *decision* to be there. I can remember standing in that tent watching that fire-eater and I swear my whole life was there; it meant everything to me.

And my friends would go with me to the Ten-in-One, but my friends were different, 'cause they took the whole show as some sort of weird challenge, and all through this fire-eater's perfect act, my friends would be talking. And they'd be saying stuff like, "Oh, I know how he does that, Penn, he just coats his mouth with something." They would try to convince me there was some sort of something you could just smear in your mouth, then go suck on a soldering iron, and it wasn't going to hurt you.

And it's not just kids—it's also adults—and it's usually a man, and it's most often a man who's with some woman he's trying desperately, and often pathetically, to impress. And I'll hear this guy who just thinks he's got to pretend to know everything, you know? So he's saying stuff like, "Oh, don't worry about him honey, he's just using cold fire." Yeah. *(He laughs)*

Or needles. Now the reason that Teller and I are working together today, is about thirteen years ago I saw Teller on stage in Jersey, alone and silently eating those needles. When I watched him up on that stage I got the same feeling in my guts that I used to get watching the fire-eater as a kid, and I knew we had to work together, and we have been ever since.

Now, I go in the lobby during intermission. I have a cola and I talk to folks and I hang out. But the whole time I'm talking, I also try to listen, and I've learned a lot from eavesdropping on you guys for all these years. And one of the things I've learned is there's a certain kind of person that comes to our show, and they may like the show, but they don't *get* it. And these are the people who cannot accept mystery.

Now I want to try to make this very clear to you: by "not accepting mystery," I am not talking about scientists, and I am not talking about skeptics. 'Cause I'm a skeptic, and I've always felt that skeptics love the mystery, and that's why they don't want to believe anything. They don't want to have any faith. They either want to have it scientifically proven over and over again, or they want to leave it alone. "We'll get to it. Let it go." The kind of people that cannot accept mystery are the kind of people that, when there's a mystery there, they just believe the first thing they're told for their whole life, or they pretend to have an open mind, so they'll believe anything that's popular that comes along, or they'll make up something that makes sense to them and they'll just believe it. Just anything that will shut the mystery out of their heads and stop them from really thinking.

And I'll hear people doing this even with things as trivial as the needles. I'll hear guys in the lobby with these real authoritative voices gathering little crowds of people going, "Oh, yeah, needles, yeah, I figured that one out, sure. He's got a little pocket sewn in the back of his throat. It's a skin graft from his leg." Or my favorite one, and I actually heard this, I did not make this up. (Some stuff I just make up, but this I heard.) There was a guy in L.A., who was talking about "candy needles." Now I don't know where this guy ever heard of candy needles, but I assume he figured they're manufactured around Halloween time, as treats for the neighborhood children. I don't know.

Anyways, about nineteen years have passed, and those kids that I grew up with, I guess they're all still living in Greenfield, Massachusetts, and I turned out to be a fire-eater, and the ironic thing I found out, is there's no trick. Not to this. To everything else in the show there's a trick—don't let anybody tell you differently. Susan floating in the air, she wasn't hypnotized—there's no "balance point." Go home, get a chair, clear your mind, think clean thoughts, concentrate: you'll break your ass. It's a gimmick, it's a lie, it's a cheat, it's a swindle! But fire-eating is a stunt, and if anybody here still thinks that there's any such thing as cold fire, and I'm using it, you wait till I get it lit, you raise your hand, I'll stick it in your eye—prove it to you.

Teller enters from left with the fire-eating props.

Teller's coming out here with a fireproof camping fuel container. In the container is lighter fluid—it's Ronson brand—and Teller's dipping the torches in.

Teller hands Penn a torch.

The torches are cotton, sewn tightly around a threaded, metal rod that's then screwed into a wooden handle. It's not the cotton that burns, it's the fuel that burns and the way fire-eating works is this:

You've got moisture throughout your mouth, and all that moisture has got to evaporate from any given part of your mouth, before that part will burn. So you learn how to handle the burning vapors, then you gotta make it look good. Now if you've got a lot of saliva in your mouth (and that's at least where I try to keep *most* of mine), you rub your lips right along the cotton and pull that vapor off. Now the vapor's still burning, but if you breathe in a little bit, the audience can't see it, so you got a beautiful surprise there. Then you just wait till the time is right and just let it flow, like it was magic smoke. Then when you want to put the fire out, there's a move for that, too, and it's the move that gives it the name "fire-eating." Now, you're not actually *eating* the flame, but I guess they figure that "Oral Fire Extinguishing" didn't sound that butch. When you feel your mouth drying out, you close your lips tightly. That cuts out most of the oxygen and . . . *(He snaps his fingers)* the fire goes out. Now when I was being taught this, I got burned every time I tried it, and I still get burned occasionally, but the burns you get from fire-eating are for the most part extremely minor. They're the kind of burns you get—you know what I'm talking about—when you eat a pizza too fast, and that cheese'll snag you, or you gulp some hot coffee. Now I'm not trying to snow you. I'm not talking no mind-over-matter jive. There's no such thing, it just hurts like holy hell. But it's not dangerous. The dangerous thing is something lay people don't even think about. And that is every time you do this act, no matter how carefully or how well, you swallow about a teaspoon of the lighter fluid, and that stuff is poisonous—that's why they write "Harmful or Fatal if Swallowed" right there on the can—and the effect is, to a certain degree, cumulative. Now I say a certain degree: I do eight shows a week, I'm a big guy, that doesn't affect me. Carnies, the real boys, they'll do up to fifty shows a day, and in as little as two or three years that stuff'll build up in their liver and they'll get sick enough, they actually have to take time off and do another line of work in the carney while that liver regenerates, which, thankfully, it will do.

Now I take the time to explain all of this to you in such detail because I think it's more fascinating to think of someone poisoning themselves to death slowly on stage than merely burning themselves, and after all, we're here to entertain you.

I really tell you this 'cause this is the last bit in the show, and when you leave here tonight and you're thinking about our show, as I hope you will be, I don't want you to be thinking about *how* we did it. I want you to be thinking about *why*. So sit back and relax, I'm going to burn myself.

Teller lights the torch. Penn twirls it with a flourish.

This move right here and this move right here are called stalling.

Penn and Teller look out at the audience, studying them.

I realize you've been sitting in these seats a long time, but if you can just bear with us another moment, we'd like to look out at you guys. 'Cause there's an obvious but still unique quality of live theatre, and that is that while we're doing the show, you're right here in the room with us. And that means light will fall on some of your faces. And if light happens to fall on one of your faces while we're doing the show we'll do a small part of the show for you, I mean, just for you, just staring right in your face. And when we do that, and we've picked you, and you know it, and you can feel it . . . we're not paying any attention to you at all. We're trying to get the tricks to work, get the laughs. We can't worry about you individually. So what I'm saying—convolutedly—is that right now is the place in the show we can look at you in the same light that we're in, and we can kinda pay attention. And it's really important. And I used to feel that importance should be made explicit, so I would do these little speeches about community and the speeches were superficial and they were contrived, and I really believed them, so they were embarrassing. So now I'm trying to learn to shut up and look at you. Teller's got it down.

And if you're the kind of person that needs to sum things up, all you need to know now is that you're in our tent, so it's okay. And the sideshow ain't dead. That's for damn sure.

Penn eats fire.

—*Penn Jillette*

The photographs in this book are reproduced with the kind permission of the following photographers, individuals or organizations: p. 2, 8, 10, 12, 13, 14, 17, 103, Jim Moore; p. 5, Friedemann Simon; p. 11, Ronald Smith; p. 19, F-stop Fitzgerald; p. 20, Agnaldo S. Maciel; p. 22, 27, 30, 33, Diane Couves; p. 38, 45, 47, 55, 80, 83, Holton Rower; p. 41, 50, 51, 52, Linda Alaniz, Martha Swope Associates; p. 56, 58, 69, The Flying Karamazov Brothers; p. 62, Laine Wilser, Goodman Theatre; p. 61, Lisa Ebright; p. 64, 65, 73, Linda Schwartz; p. 74, 76, 88, Francois Rivard, Cirque du Soleil; p. 84, Denis Lacombe; p. 90, 93, 94, 99, Avner the Eccentric; p. 104, 107, 108, 111, 112, 113, 115, 116, 118, 121, Terry Lorant; p. 122, 138, Nancy Campbell; p. 126, Clem Fiore; p. 129, The Wooster Group; p. 132, 133, Massimo Agus; p. 143, 154, 155, 159, 161, Fred Stimson; p. 162, Janet L. Knott; p. 165, 168, 173, 174, Penn and Teller.